JESUS CHRIST

JESUS CHRIST

The Man from Nazareth and the Exalted Lord

*The 1984 Sizemore Lectures
in Biblical Studies
at Midwestern Baptist
Theological Seminary*

by
EDUARD SCHWEIZER

edited by
HULITT GLOER

MERCER
University Press

ISBN 0-86554-225-2 (cloth)
ISBN 0-86554-226-0 (paper)

Jesus Christ: The Man from Nazareth and the Exalted Lord
Copyright © 1987
Mercer University Press, Macon, Georgia 31207

The paper used in this publication meets
the minimum requirements of American National Standard
for Information Sciences—Permanence of Paper
for Printed Library Materials, ANSI Z39.48-1984.

Library of Congress Cataloging-in-Publication Data
Eduard Schweizer, 1913–
Jesus Christ, the man from Nazareth and the Exalted Lord

    Includes bibliographical references and index.
    1. Jesus Christ—Person and offices.
2. Jesus Christ—History of doctrines—Early church, ca. 30-600.
3. Jesus Christ—History of doctrines—20th century.
4. Schweizer, Eduard, 1913–   . I. Gloer, Hulitt.
II. Title. III. Title: Sizemore lectures in biblical studies.
BT202.S38   1987   232   86-33268
ISBN 0-86554-225-2 (alk. paper)
ISBN 0-86554-226-0 (pbk. : alk. paper)

55, 988

CONTENTS

PREFACE

In November 1984 Midwestern Baptist Theological Seminary asked me to deliver the Sizemore Lectures. As I was just preparing my long article "Jesus Christus" for *Theologische Realenzyklopädie*, I decided to deal with the Christological problem in the New Testament. I set out to present a shorter, less detailed version of the dictionary article more keyed to seminary students and educated laymen interested in theological problems. The week in Kansas City was one of the very best in the forty-five years of married life that have been granted to Elizabeth and myself—not merely because of the high quality of Kansas City steaks and the restaurants in which we were invited to eat them, but even much more because of an extraordinarily friendly welcome in the Seminary community. It was also the Seminary's wish to have these lectures published. This week was only possible because of a previous invitation from Acadia Theological College in Wolfville, Nova Scotia, where I delivered the same series of lectures at the end of October, again in a most friendly and truly Christian atmosphere—there, unfortunately, without my wife accompanying me.

In February 1985 my former student, professor Ulrich Luz in Berne, Switzerland, asked me to describe in as personal a way as possible in a guest lecture my experience with Rudolf Bultmann. This led to a short autobiography, published later in *Evangelische Theologie* 45 (1985): 322-37. I have rewritten and greatly enlarged it in English to add it to the Sizemore Lectures because I am more and more of the opinion that theological reflections always mirror the experience of their author and should be seen against his or her life to become really alive.

I am extremely grateful to Professor Hulitt Gloer at Midwestern who took the time and trouble to edit this book and to smooth my English style. Moreover, my thanks go to Acadia College and Midwestern Seminary as well as to Mercer University Press for kindly accepting my manuscript for publication. The reader will also realize how much the years of companionship with Elizabeth have contributed to it.

Männedorf (Zurich), 7 October 1985   Eduard Schweizer

Chapter 1

MODERN APPROACHES TO CHRISTOLOGY[1]

(a) Bultmann and His First Critics

The fascination with *Rudolf Bultmann*'s theology in the 1930s lay in the fact that he offered his students both the unlimited freedom of historical-critical research (which every historian would consider indispensable for his work) and a full belief in the central Christological creedal formulae of the New Testament and the later church. While agreeing with liberal "lives of Jesus" that portrayed Jesus as a teacher and prophet, he thought that the liberal scholars were, by and large, not consistent or thoroughgoing enough and that they tended to read into the text whatever religious or ethical views they considered important. Bultmann went so far as to declare that the cry of the crucified Jesus may, in fact, have been a cry of extreme despair. Most significant for Bultmann was the recognition that according to all books of the New Testament (with the possible exception of James and Jude) Easter was the decisive event. In the days after Easter the disciples perceived that Jesus *was indeed* God's messiah. Whether Jesus thought himself to be the messiah, therefore, is not important. It may, after all, have belonged to the status of his humiliation that he did not know of his messiahship, even as, for instance, he did not know that the earth was round. The only important fact is that he *was* (or rather *is*) the messiah, and this was disclosed to his disciples in the days after Easter.

Rational thinking cannot go behind the Easter event. We can believe or disbelieve. The disciples' proclamation of Jesus as the Christ of God may convince us, leave us untouched, or prompt conscious rejection. Still it is their "kerygma into which Jesus has risen,"[2] and the center of this kerygma is the

---

[1]See Eduard Schweizer, "Jesusdarstellungen und Christologien seit Rudolf Bultmann," in *Rudolf Bultmanns Werk und Wirkung* (Darmstadt: Wissenschaftliche Buchgesellschaft, 1984) 122-48.

[2]Rudolf Bultmann, "Das Verhältnis der urchristlichen Christusbotschaft zum historischen Jesus," *Sitzungsberichte der Heidelberger Akademie der Wissenschaften, philosoph.-histor. Klaße* (Heidelberg: C. Winter, 1960) 27; reprinted in Bultmann, *Exegetica* (Tübingen: J. C. B. Mohr, 1967) 469.

doctrine of justification by faith, the message that man never finds his real life in his own work, in what he performs and accomplishes, but only in its giveness, in what he receives and accepts as a gift. Thus, it is the kerygma, the post-Easter preaching of the church, that changes our wrong self-understanding into faith in the grace of God.

Bultmann did not deny that there was some continuity between Jesus' work (his deeds and his preaching) on the one hand and the proclamation of the church on the other hand. He even spoke of an implicit Christology[3] in the earthly ministry of Jesus. Nevertheless, since we believe because the Spirit of God has conquered our wrong thinking, not because we are historically sure that a man named Jesus of Nazareth has uttered this or that statement, it is of no avail to investigate how much or how little of the so-called teaching of Jesus really goes back to Jesus himself. It is the church that discovered that Jesus, in his death on the cross, where all human self-made works ended and nothing except the grace of God remained, was, indeed, the messiah, who enables men to be freed from trusting their belief in their own works and open to accepting God's grace. It is this kerygma that, in the power of the Holy Spirit, convinces the hearer to abandon his trust in his own strength and to accept the message of justification by grace. Thus, Jesus is indeed the Christ, the Son of God, one with the Father and the Holy Spirit, and total trust in grace is the true and everlasting life.

While still a student of Bultmann I asked him why, then, we needed Jesus. Once we become convinced that this message of the total preponderance of grace is the right view of man and his life, why should we still remember and remind others that it was Jesus whose destiny led for the first time to this insight? I acknowledged Bultmann's insistence that man is so deeply involved in trusting in his own work that he needs the event of Jesus' life and death, not merely a theoretical philosophy, to change his mind. According to this view, however, Jesus is little more than a motivation. After some hesitation, Bultmann accepted the term "motivation," but, one is forced to ask, is this term sufficient to describe adequately the significance of Jesus?

In 1953 *Ernst Käsemann* attacked Bultmann's position[4] as a belief in one's own believing. Is there really no other basis for our belief than the fact that the disciples believed in the days after Easter around A.D. 30? Käsemann suggested (as Karl Barth had earlier stated) that faith is basically and eminently interested in the *extra nos*, in God's existence and action "outside of us," in

---

[3]Bultmann, "Verhältnis," 15-16, and Bultmann, *Theologie des Neuen Testaments*, 9th ed. (Tübingen: J. C. B. Mohr, 1984) 456-57; repeated by many others (cf. Schweizer, "Jesusdarstellungen," 123, n4).

[4]Ernst Käsemann, "Das Problem des historischen Jesus," in *Exegetische Versuche und Besinnungen*, 2 vols. (Göttingen: Vandenhoeck und Ruprecht, 1967) 1:187-214; cf. "Sackgassen im Streit um den historischen Jesus" in *Exegetische Versuche* 2:31-68, and Bruno Forte, *Jesus von Nazaret: Geschichte Gottes—Gott der Geschichte* (Tübingen: Tübinger Theologische Studien 22, 1984) 102-105.

salvation that is not at our disposal, a salvation that has happened before us and according to God's free, contingent will, unconditioned by our behavior and attitude (though this may become essential in a secondary stage). Shortly afterward, *Gerhard von Rad* insisted in his theology of the Old Testament[5] that God was to be found in history, even contingent history (history not forced by casual events or human deeds), not in ideas, systems, and philosophies.

Thus, the Achilles' heel of Bultmann's theology became more and more visible: it is not possible to reduce the existence of Jesus on earth to a mere "that," to the mere fact of his death. A death in a home for the elderly surrounded by friends, flowers, and chocolates would have been a totally different event. Even a crucifixion after fifty years of successful work in the midst of an imposing group of followers would have been very different. Even if we went one step further and spoke of the crucifixion of a Jew of thirty years of age, would it really help as long as we did not ask *who* this Jew was? If he had been a revolutionary who could see the victory of his revolution, though in its death throes the conquered enemy succeeded still in killing him, or if he had been a masochist who longed for a spectacular martyrdom, it would have been totally different. Thus the question of Jesus' identity is an indispensable one.

How then are we to answer this question? Recent attempts have demonstrated two quite different, though often related, directions. Most scholars have concentrated their interest on the earthly Jesus. Unlike the lives of Jesus that had been written at the end of the last and the beginning of this century—often in a rather imaginative way—these scholars have attempted to find the central kerygma of the post-Easter church in the earthly ministry of Jesus. More importantly, they have attempted to understand the whole of his life itself as "kerygma," as a message that cannot be understood by a detached neutral scrutiny, but only by a personal involvement in what is detected in Jesus. The emphasis in this approach focuses on the earthly Jesus, on the authority of his word and work that led people to believe in his message and assured them of God's grace (or, in a more unreligious term, of the givenness of life) and incited them to obey him and to build a new world after his vision. The other approach is the attempt to define, in different ways, what has been objectively changed by the life, death, and resurrection of Jesus, apart from what his believers achieved in their faithful obedience to him. The emphasis would, in this case, focus on the death and resurrection rather than on the words and deeds of Jesus.

(b) The Interest in Jesus of Nazareth

I shall first examine the new interest in the earthly Jesus. Several approaches are possible. *Jewish scholars* stress Jesus' continuity with the Old Testament. They remind us that Jesus and his contemporary Jewish hearers did not think in terms of metaphysics. Even if Jesus had spoken of "the Father" and "the Son," it would only have illustrated his function, his dependence on

---

[5]Gerhard von Rad, *Old Testament Theology*, 2 vols. (New York: Harper and Row, 1962, 1965) 2:356-87.

and his obedience to God, in the same way that the people of Israel or its king could be called "son of God."[6] Jesus was a Jewish teacher, with some of the characteristics of a prophet, who called Israel back to an obedience to the law in which the innermost meaning of God's commandments, their "spirit," was more important than the letter. Quite a number of these scholars admit that there was something in his person, message, and work that went beyond the qualifications of a teacher or even a prophet.[7] Still, he never asked people to believe *in* him, but tried to make them believe in God in the same way that he believed in God.[8] According to this approach, his death was the end of his efficacy,[9] except for the effect that his memory had on later generations, as in a similar fashion the old Israel is still effective in the modern state of Israel.[10] While it is obvious that the New Testament means more than this when it speaks of the resurrection, we must remember with a deep sense of shame what Christians have done to Jews, and seriously respect their way of believing without trying to obscure differences. Time and again, new developments took place in Israel's history and the Christian church thinks that this has happened in an outstanding way in the coming of Jesus. As a Jewish partner in the ongoing Jewish-Christian dialogue once observed, "To speak of Jesus makes sense for a Christian only if he speaks of him as the Christ, the Logos, and the Son of God."[11]

Herbert Braun described the life of Jesus in much the same way as Bultmann himself would have done. For Braun, the decisive difference lies in the fact that Jesus' life is the kerygma itself, to which the Easter event adds nothing new. "Resurrection" is merely a historical—and, today, obsolete—expression to describe the authority that the earthly Jesus exercised on those who followed him.[12] Clearly Bultmann accepted Braun's approach to a great extent, for Bultmann had himself reckoned with an implicit Christology in Jesus' words and deeds, and Braun detects in them exactly the same kerygma of justification by faith that the post-Easter church proclaimed. It is, therefore, an understanding of man that marks the continuity of the New Testament message, whereas Christologies may vary and are "electives" rather than obligatory expressions

---

[6]Cf. Martin Buber, *Zwei Glaubensweisen* (Zurich: Manesse Verlag, 1950), 5-11.

[7]Pinchas Lapide, in Pinchas Lapide and Ulrich Luz, *Der Jude Jesus* (Zurich: Benziger, 1979) 117; Schalom Ben-Chorin, *Jesus im Judentum* (Wuppertal: Theologischer Verlag, 1970) 22, 42; see also Buber, *Zwei Glaubenweisen*.

[8]Lapide, *Der Jude Jesus*, 117; Ben-Chorin, *Jesus*, 51.

[9]David Flusser, "Jesus in Selbstzeugnissen und Bilddokumenten," *Rowolts Monographien* 140 (1968): 133.

[10]Ben-Chorin, *Jesus*, 79.

[11]Quoted by Erich Grässer, "Christen und Juden," *Pastoraltheologie* 71 (1982): 438 (my translation).

[12]Herbert Braun, *Jesus* (Stuttgart: Kreuz-Verlag, 1969) 154.

of faith.[13] In an impressive way Braun shows how Jesus gave men the freedom to see themselves as accepted and loved and instituted in them in this way the capacity of loving others. "I am given, and I am asked to love" is the center of the Jesus event. It is even what the term "God" means: "When you have seen your brother, you have seen God."[14] How far is such a view from the old liberal research on the life of Jesus,[15] or even from the Greeks, who detected that love was an outstandingly important human phenomenon and, therefore, created the god Eros or the goddess Aphrodite? No wonder John Calvin thought that the human mind was a perpetually running idol factory.[16]

Whereas Braun speaks of the individual love of one's neighbor, *Dorothee Sölle* stresses the social and political aspects of love. To her, it is indisputable that we are living in the posttheistic age. While Jewish monographs emphasize Jesus' proclamation of the true God without speaking of his divine sonship, Sölle, conversely, sees in Jesus the definitive representative of God who now takes his place. Whatever God used to be to man in former times, *Jesus* is now. God is now exclusively living in the Jesus-event. Jesus opens God's future and plays his role, a role that nobody else could play.[17] Thus, God is dependent on humanity because human beings give Jesus a continuing efficacy by doing what he urged them to do.[18] In a society without class distinctions, Sölle contends, God would in some sense become alive again, since "resurrection" means nothing other than "the newly won identity of all men."[19] Both Braun and Sölle speak in deep seriousness and concern of the death of God and his representation by Jesus. But in these views Jesus is little more than a consul general who keeps up appearances by representing a country that has ceased to exist.

Braun's emphasis on conversion or, to use Bultmann's terminology, the change of the individual's self-understanding is taken up by *Kurt Niederwimmer*. He questions, however, the use of existential terminology, since it covers

---

[13]Herbert Braun, "Der Sinn der neutestamentlichen Christologie," *Zeitschrift für Theologie und Kirche* 54 (1957): 368, 370-71; explicitly accepted by R. Bultmann, *Verhältnis*, 22.

[14]Herbert Braun, "Die Problematik einer Theologie des Neuen Testaments," *Zeitschrift für Theologie und Kirche* 57 (1960): 18, reprinted in *Gesammelte Studien zum Neuen Testament und seiner Umwelt* (Tübingen: J. C. B. Mohr, 1962) 341; Braun, "Gottes Existenz und meine Geschichtlichkeit im Neuen Testament," in Erich Dinkler, ed., *Zeit und Geschichte* [Festschrift für Rudolf Bultmann] (Tübingen: J. C. B. Mohr, 1964) 418-21.

[15]Erich Grässer, *Verkündigung und Forschung* 18/2 (1973): 14.

[16]John Calvin, *Institutes of the Christian Religion*, 2 vols., trans. Henry Betteridge (Grand Rapids: William B. Eerdmanns, 1957) 1:97.

[17]Dorothee Sölle, *Stellvertretung: ein Kapitel Theologie nach dem "Tode Gottes"* (Stuttgart: Kreuz-Verlag, 1967) 175, 181, 190.

[18]Ibid., 194, 204-205.

[19]Ibid., 170; cf. 181, 200.

only the rational side of man (his conscious thinking, his philosophizing) while his subconscious life is probably much more decisive. This subconscious life expresses itself in mythological language. Demythologizing, therefore, robs the text of its most important features if it means more than bringing the unconscious roots of our language into the open.[20] The crisis that becomes visible in Jesus is a process of change in the collective conflict of conscious beliefs with unconscious convictions differing from them. In Jesus, a new God and a new man become real. God is no longer the Jewish God of the law, but a different God, since man is now, according to Mark 2:27, the measure and standard of the law.[21] While Braun suggests that accepting oneself *is* the phenomenon that in the Bible is called "grace" or "forgiveness," Niederwimmer can say that finding oneself is the kingdom of God.[22]

In the wake of this approach, *Hanna Wolff* attempted to analyze the psyche of Jesus, a task Niederwimmer considered impossible. She finds in him the ideally integrated man, in whom male and female characteristics are united. He is the mediator, therefore, who provides his believers with a basic trust and a feeling of being sheltered.[23] He could not be truly human without a personal "shadow," namely, his inability to separate himself clearly from apocalypticism, to draw social and political conclusions and to be totally open even to animals and their sufferings.[24]

Social and political activity rather than individual conversion are emphasized in the Marxist books about Jesus. Very impressive by his personal involvement and honesty is *Milan Machovec*. While the question of God's existence is of no importance to Machovec, and the dogma of atheism is as questionable as the dogma of theism, he recognizes that science alone does not provide an adequate basis for ethics, and that socioeconomic developments can lead to falsehood as well as to truth. He acknowledges that Marxist governments have not created a paradise without class distinctions any more than churches have realized the kingdom of God. Hence dialogue between Marxists and Christians is possible and can be helpful for both.[25] In the Old Testament God is not the God of nature and of the law of causation, but the God of address, who calls men to activity. He is always the coming God, opening the dimension of the future, awakening in humanity critical social questions and revolutionary visions. For Jesus also, the future shapes the present, and this

---

[20]Kurt Niederwimmer, *Jesus* (Göttingen: Vandenhoeck und Ruprecht, 1968) 24, 45, 48.

[21]Ibid., 51, 66, 82, 69.

[22]Braun, *Jesus*, 168-69; Niederwimmer, *Jesus*, 88.

[23]Hanna Wolff, *Jesus, der Mann*, 3rd ed. (Stuttgart: *Radius-Verlag*, 1977) 70, 82, 166.

[24]Ibid., 139-40, 141, 149, 154-55.

[25]Milan Machovec, *A Marxist Looks at Jesus* (Philadelphia: Fortress, 1976) 25-27, 35, 38.

future is already embodied in him, though it is man who will have to realize it. The belief in the resurrection of Jesus has been caused by the experience of the Spirit. Moved by the Spirit, Peter reinterpreted the hopes the disciples had cherished before Easter so that Easter was born out of Pentecost, and while this reflected a genuine experience for the disciples, it precipitated a new interpretation of the earthly ministry of Jesus in light of his death.[26]

More aggressive is *Fernando Belo*'s structuralistic and materialistic analysis of the gospel of Mark. According to Belo, two different systems dominated Israel. The first was the system of pure/impure, which allowed the ruling class of the priests, closely connected with the royal court in Jerusalem, to become indispensable, since they alone were able to purify the impure. The second was the system of gift/guilt in which God alone is judging and forgiving. This system was proclaimed by the lower class of the Levites in the North and the prophets. Whereas the priests stress the power of God in the past (the covenant on Mount Sinai and its law), the Levites emphasize the coming God and are open to new prophetic stories.[27] Jesus sides with the latter view in his "practice of the hands" (his *love*), "of the feet" (his *hope* for an expansion of God's kingdom even to the Gentiles), and "of the eyes" (his *faith*, which interprets what happens in an "analyzing lecture"). Real "demythologization" is only possible within historical materialism, because the bourgeois interpretation of Bultmann and his school dissolves real history into a timeless inwardness and sees only the heart of man instead of seeing that conversion of the heart must lead to liberation of the body. Jesus was a radical communist whose renunciation of violence was merely strategic.[28]

A church that knows how shamefully often it did *not* work and fight and suffer for social and political justice and betterment should have open ears for these authors who remind us of the priority of obeying God before discussing theoretically his existence or nonexistence. Still we are forced to ask whether Christology and soteriology merely mean that man "finds himself?" Is not God more than a symbol of the new being of a human person who has overcome the killing demands of the law or integrated male and female qualities in his or her psyche or love in its more individual or more collective dimension? As soon as we ask where the roots of all our activity—or nonactivity—lie, we can no longer evade the God question. What or who gives us the strength that enables us to do anything, the "indicative" that opens the way to the "imperative?" Why should we fight for the weak in a world in which the law of Darwin decrees that only the strong will survive? What or who causes us to engage in that unreasonable fight? And who or what provides new strength when we fail? Further: who or what opens our eyes to the truth? No doubt, the church has to

---

[26]Ibid., 53-59, 64-66, 88-93, 165-66, 171.

[27]Fernando Belo, *Das Markusevangelium materialistisch gelesen* (Stuttgart: Alektor Verlag, 1980) 79-83.

[28]Ibid., 306-16, 323-24, 353-54, 325-29.

learn from many people outside of it that charity is not always helpful but may also veil the rights of the poor. And yet who or what shows us what is really good? History is never unambiguous. Jeremiah had to announce that the defeat of Israel was God's will and, therefore, good in the deepest sense of the word. And in an extreme way, this happened again on the cross of Jesus. It is, according to the Bible, the faithfulness of God alone that carries us through all our defeats and opens us to the real truth. It is not the strength or even the power of the church that proclaims the truth of God's existence. It is its weakness and helplessness needing his intervention, his leadership, his help.

(c) The Interest in the Kerygma of the Church

When we turn to the second type of approach, *Karl Rahner* is an outstanding example of a radical emphasis on the objective change in the world effected by the Christ-event. Rahner's notion of "anonymous Christians"—who know that all questions about who man is must, by necessity, transcend one's own being—is similar to Bultmann's thesis that there is a preliminary understanding of God outside of the Christian faith. Thus, even as one may have some knowledge of what a friend is, but not *really* know what a friend is until one has found a friend, so one may have some knowledge of God but not really know God until one finds God. Rahner starts from the premise that within the unimaginably long evolution of the world the period since the origin of a human person is a very short but decisive one. Within it, Jesus Christ, God and man in one, reveals the state for which all men are destined, the goal of all evolution.[29] Through him history has become irreversible for in his message and person God was present in a unique way. From now on history moves toward its fulfillment when all human beings will become like Christ. Even though salvation history is not directly visible because of the fact of human sin, it is coexistent and coextensive but not identical with world history. Therefore, within it "an official, churchly, and pure salvation history" is to be distinguished.[30] While this is a very imposing approach, certain questions remain to be asked. How far is the risen Christ identical with that history of the true church? How far is he still "over-against" it? Is it possible to see the history of mankind from the perspective of evolution, if we mean by it more than physical development? Is a history in which sin plays an important role, a history under the shadow of the cross, to be compared with physical evolution, in which only some contingent catastrophes may slow down the pace of progress?

If we cannot follow Rahner's view and its model (the vision of *Teilhard de Chardin*), should we not combine both approaches in some way? The question is, of course, in *what* way? Shall we start from the earthly ministry of Jesus (Braun and others) or from the post-Easter kerygma (Bultmann and others)? The first way seems to commend itself. Who would not want to go back to Je-

---

[29]Karl Rahner, *Grundkurs des Glaubens* (Freiburg: Herder, 1982) 170-93.

[30]Ibid., 194-98, 244-51, 188-95, 159, 165.

sus, as he really was, and learn afresh what he wanted to convey to us? And who would not fear that, otherwise, Christianity would become a mere ideology,[31] the dogma of which is merely repeated while having no relevance for the modern world? Many have approached the problem in this way, and it is impossible to do more than mention briefly a few names.

Ernst Fuchs shows how, by justifying tax collectors and prostitutes, Jesus dared to act as if he were God himself,[32] and how his whole life interpreted his words so that they, like the sacrament, created faith and brought about a real change in Jesus' hearers. Thus, Jesus is the word of God itself.[33] In this way, Fuchs presupposes the kerygma of the church, but plays down the importance of the resurrection of Jesus. It was not lack of faith that caused the flight of the disciples, but merely the fact that they did not yet possess the Spirit, and the Easter visions were simply a rebirth of the expectations of an imminent parousia, as John the Baptist (not Jesus!) had taught it.[34]

Karl-Heinz Ohlig sees in Jesus *the* archetype of real humanity. In Israel, history manifests a personal structure. It is not evolution or progress. It is shaped by the sociopolitical engagement of God on the one side and the nonsense of a multitude of demons on the other. History's problems are answered in human terms, not from somewhere beyond the stars. Jesus'uniqueness is the central reduction of all answers to the basic human problems. His resurrection means his confirmation, and the transcendental dimension of the biblical language expresses the impossibility of manipulating life.[35] The problem with approaches such as these is whether, in light of the testimony of the New Testament, we can restrict the meaning of the resurrection of Jesus in this way.

This may also be true of *Edward Schillebeeckx*, who focuses on the post-Easter period. Jesus and the movement that he created are always to be seen together.[36] The continuity consists in the fact that time and time again different groups found salvation in Jesus, whose life by its nature and quality caused the typical reaction of faith. But what about the variety of expressions this faith takes? To declare all dogmatic interpretations within the New Testament or even beyond it right is no solution; even if this were true, one would have to

---

[31]Cf. Ernst Fuchs, *Jesus, Wort und Tat* (Tübingen: J. C. B. Mohr, 1971) 44. "The question of the historical Jesus is *the* antiphilosophical question" (my translation); see also ch. 5, §i.

[32]Ernst Fuchs, *Zur Frage nach dem historischen Jesus*, Gesammelte Aufsätze 2 (Tübingen: J. C. B. Mohr, 1965) 156.

[33]Fuchs, *Jesus*, 40, 70, 73, 84, 105, 107, 121.

[34]Ibid., 116; Fuchs, *Zur Frage*, 396.

[35]Karl-Heinz Ohlig, *Jesus, Entwurf zum Menschsein* (Stuttgart: KBW-Verlag, 1974) 56, 100, 18, 22, 24, 31, 38, 79.

[36]Edward Schillebeeckx, *Jesus, Die Geschichte von einem Lebenden* (Freiburg: Herder, 1980) 38-41; *Christus und die Christen, Die Geschichte einer neuen Lebenspraxis* (Freiburg: Herder, 1980) 612-13.

set priorities and emphases. Nor does a canon within the canon or a reference to authentic words and deeds of Jesus help, since these would need interpretation.[37] Therefore, the only possible approach is that of a permanently swinging pendulum that goes from the biblical interpretations of Jesus to modern disclosures and back again.[38] Easter is the experience in which the disciples, who had not really lost their faith, experience conversion as they learn to "see" that in spite of his death which seemed to leave no hope, God had indeed acted in Jesus. Schillebeeckx emphasizes that this "seeing" was given by the risen Lord and was not merely created by the psyches of the disciples themselves. "Resurrection" was the Jewish term of that time to express the fact that Jesus was still living.[39] Again, we might ask whether, in this view, Christ does not become identical with the church, though in quite a different way from Rahner's view, since the variety of these disclosures (and not one official church view) is emphasized and the earthly Jesus remains the decisive criterion for Schillebeeckx.

An emphasis on modern disclosures is especially apparent in the challenge of *Liberation Theology* which comes to us from our Latin American and African colleagues.[40] In their view, Bultmann was right in refuting any ideas of understanding the biblical message without personal involvement, but this is true not so much in terms of the individual as in terms of political and social involvement. It is not possible to understand Jesus as long as a person is detached from the problems, the misery, the ardent desires and dreams of his or her surroundings. The question that must be raised is whether these needs and visions serve to enable us to understand the Christological answers of the New Testament, or whether Christology simply serves to ornament the answers given by these needs and visions themselves. There exists, however, for many of these authors, a real interest in Christology and an honest effort to listen to the biblical answers.[41]

---

[37]Schillebeeckx, *Jesus*, 48-49, 542, 46-48.

[38]Schillebeeckx, *Christus*, 69.

[39]Schillebeeckx, *Jesus*, 338-40, 344-50, 571, 576.

[40]Gustavo Gutierrez, *Theologie der Befreiung* (Munich: Kaiser, 1976); Norbert Greinacher, *Die Kirche der Armen. Zur Theologie der Befreiung* (Munich: Piper, 1980) 152: "The future of the theology of liberation may decide the destiny of the church" (my translation); Claus Bussmann, *Befreiung durch Jesus?* (Munich: Piper, 1980) 159-60: "Christology is, today, impossible without consciously being aware of the reality of human society" (my translation). See additional references in my article "Jesus Christus" in *Theologische Realenzyklopädie*, §1.11.3.

[41]Bussman, *Befreiung*, 40. 60, 158: "Jesus claims the whole man, not merely his political liberation, and Christology cannot be reduced to what is just useful to political activity, though, conversely, no real knowledge of Christ is thinkable without close touch to such activity." See also the warnings in Karl Lehmann, *Theologie der Befreiung* (Einsiedeln: Johannes Verlag, 1977) 31-32, 36-37.

Process Theology, stamped by Whitehead's cosmological philosophy,[42] tries to express Christology in terms of the modern insights of science. There is no longer anything like matter; everything has become life, event, "actual occasion," "pulsation" and, therefore, also growth.[43] God, as the act of creativity, is, consistent with his very being, enriched by the reactions of his creatures. This becomes understandable if and when we see God as trinitarian, loving and being loved within himself. God, loving as the Father his son and being loved by him in the power of the Spirit, is the instantiation of the principle of being itself. Such an understanding allows us to see in God the creator not only of individuals, but also of societies, since he is bearing in himself the structure of togetherness, of love and reaction to love.[44] Thus, a Christology that would take Jesus of Nazareth seriously would understand him as (the trinitarian) "God's supreme act of self-expression."[45] The problem is understanding what this means.

According to *Schubert Ogden*, God did not act toward Jesus differently from the way he acts toward any man, but Jesus' reception was different. He really understood God and interpreted his acts rightly. This would, again, lead to a Christology in which the behavior of Jesus, exemplary for all his followers, would be emphasized. According to *David R. Griffin*, however, God's intention with Jesus, not merely its reception by Jesus, is different from what he intends with regard to any other being and Jesus' experience is different from what any other being might experience.[46] The same is true of *John B. Cobb*'s effort to see the Logos of God as the center of Jesus' human personality and to combine in this way God's free initiative and Jesus' free reaction to it. Emphasis is, therefore, shifted away from thinking in terms of timeless substance to a Christology understood in terms of dynamic event.[47] The objective act of God is seen as being different from other acts, even apart from its primary reception by Jesus and its secondary reception by believers. If we accept this, we are at least able to speak of God in the imagery of a person encountering other persons.

In a challenging way, *Frans Jozef van Beeck* combines a pronounced interest in the earthly ministry of Jesus with an emphasis on his resurrection. Pleading compassionately for more patience with and interest in human concerns

---

[42]Alfred North Whitehead, *Process and Reality: An Essay in Cosmology* (London: Cambridge University Press, 1929).

[43]David R. Griffin, *A Process Christology* (Philadelphia: Westminster Press, 1973) 168.

[44]Joseph Bracken, "Ein Beispiel, wie die westliche Theologie die Modernität ernstnehmen kann: die Prozess-Theologie," *Concilium Einsiedeln* 20 (1984): 38-43.

[45]Griffin, *Process*, 206.

[46]Ibid., 212-23.

[47]John B. Cobb, *Christ in a Pluralistic Age* (Philadelphia: Westminster Press, 1975) 172; cf. 138-39, 144, 170-71.

and views that may lead to new Christological discernments, he argues against a frozen classical Christology, which leaves the world caught in misery and violence, and calls for a closer touch with natural language use.[48] As Christology is the direct act of faith and the fruit of the Spirit in lives that proclaim the Christ in imitation of the earthly Jesus, it is from the beginning only possible as a response to the risen Christ in whom the earthly Jesus comes to the believer.[49]

(d) Conclusions

With Griffin, Cobb, and van Beeck, we have actually moved to the group of those who start from the post-Easter kerygma that proclaims the specific, eschatological act of God in Jesus Christ. As I see it, this is the way the New Testament speaks of Jesus. In all four gospels, in all the letters (with the possible exception of James and Jude) and in the Book of Revelation, Jesus is primarily the crucified and risen Lord. There may have been reports of miracles of Jesus and collections of logia, but they have been inserted in our canonical gospels. The idea of reverting to those good days in Galilee, wandering with Jesus and detecting in him God, is a romantic illusion. The disciples did *not* understand him then, and the way back to Galilee was only possible after the angel proclaimed him as the risen one they would encounter there (Mark 16:6-7). It is the early church that found in the New Testament writings the definitive answer to all its problems. Thus, the main question is that of the canon, regardless of our view of the process by which that canon came to exist. If we begin with the canon, and in my opinion that is what we must do, Bultmann's emphasis on beginning with the New Testament kerygma is on target. The problem that we encounter at this point is the diversity of the very different kerygmata reflected in the New Testament, a diversity in which the only common denominator is the belief that Jesus is the Christ.[50] This shows that in the same way as "Christ" defines "Jesus" as the one in whom God encounters us definitively as the savior who loves us, "Jesus" also defines "Christ" as a crucified man, not as a political or military victor or an unsurpassable miracle worker or as the wisest of all teachers of the law. Therefore, the earthly Jesus is, indeed, the criterion of all faith, provided that (1) his crucifixion and his encounter with the disciples after Easter is emphatically included, and that (2) the kerygma of God's unique presence in him is the basis of our approach.

Even if we still distinguish rationally economic and immanent trinity, we can no longer separate them. When I ask who a person is, I am not interested

---

[48]Frans Jozef van Beeck, *Christ Proclaimed—Christology as Rhetoric* (New York: Paulist Press, 1979) 507-12, 520.

[49]Ibid., 508, 573. The movement from the resurrection, as the basis of Christology, to the earthly Jesus, is also typical of Forte, *Jesus von Nazaret*, 59, 97-125. A good survey on other modern approaches is given by John A. Ziesler, *The Jesus Question* (Guildford: Lutterworth Press, 1980) 120-32.

[50]James D. G. Dunn, *Unity and Diversity in the New Testament* (London: SCM Press, 1977) 371, 376.

in physical facts (so many gallons of water, pounds of fat, and so on), but in his or her life (from what background he or she comes, what his or her calling is, how he or she behaves, and so on). Therefore, when we ask who Jesus is, we ask in what way God lives in his life and death, acts in his acts and experiences, speaks in his words and gestures. The event of his resurrection is, therefore, not an event *sui generis*. When we interpret his table fellowship not merely as a breaking down of social barriers but as the realizing of God's forgiving grace, we transcend all worldly experience and understanding in the same way as when we interpret his appearances to the disciples as those of the one who has been raised from the dead by God himself. The only difference lies in the fact that sin and death have exercised their power definitively in the crucifixion of Jesus, that the total alienation from God of all men, including those that followed him as his disciples, and the total blindness to God's life-giving grace of all men has become obvious. Therefore, as *Eberhard Jüngel*[51] has suggested, it was only through the death of God's son and his resurrection that the relation of the father to his son became analogous with what is true for the believer. In this sense, Jesus had to go through that experience as our representative.

On the one hand, we cannot speak of any detail of the earthly ministry of Jesus without deciding whether or not we see in it God's definitive act of salvation in the sense of the post-Easter kerygma. There is no description of the earthly Jesus that would not include the faith response[52] or its rejection. On the other hand, we cannot say that Jesus is the Christ without the knowledge of who he was in his earthly existence. The earliest Christian creedal formulae (for example, 1 Corinthians 15:3-5) are already summaries of history understood in terms of faith: Christ was crucified —buried—raised and seen by Cephas and the twelve, and all this happened according to the Scriptures for our sins. Even if we cannot be sure of many historical details, it seems to me that on the whole the tradition gives us an astonishingly clear picture of Jesus' person and work. This, by the way, is true for all knowledge of the past, though in varying degrees. Even when film exists, a film in which the overall picture is doubtlessly clear, we cannot be completely sure of many of the details. Therefore, Christian faith has to move like a pendulum from the proclamation of Jesus as Christ (which challenges us to look first at him) to the tradition about his whole work and experience up to his death and the experiences of his disciples, and from there to their understanding of his coming as that of the risen Lord and thus back to the testimony of the church. It is of no primary importance whether we move from Jesus to his proclamation as Christ or rather the other way round. I vote for starting with an emphasis on the Christological approaches found in the kerygma of the post-Easter church lest we confound hu-

---

[51]Eberhard Jüngel, *Gott als Geheimnis der Welt* (Tübingen: J. C. B. Mohr, 1977) 502-503, 529.

[52]Ziesler, *Jesus Question*, 124, referring to Oscar Cullmann and Norman Pittenger; see also Griffin, *Process*, 197-98.

man ideas, projects and achievements, which we can also detect in Jesus of Nazareth, with God. To be sure, Christianity can become a mere ideology, if we repeat the dogmata of the church without letting the earthly Jesus challenge our systems. By the same token, it can also become a mere ideology, if we praise the human person of Jesus and actually mean the personal or social or political visions that we have projected on him.

Chapter 2

KERYGMATIC ANSWERS
IN THE NEW TESTAMENT

(a) Jesus Christ: the (Coming and Present) Lord of the Church

The oldest confession of faith is probably to be found in the simple formula "Jesus Christ." It says that a man whose name is known is God's definitive and saving coming to the world. Later creedal formulae interpret this combination of a name and a title. It appears that the first of these formulae emphasize Jesus' resurrection, or more precisely, God's act of raising him: "If you confess with your lips that Jesus Christ is Lord and believe in your heart that God raised him from the dead, you will be saved" (Rom 10:9). Two points are essential. First, resurrection means installation as Lord. This is lordship over the church, not primarily over the universe or over the demons, as the interpretation of Paul in Romans 10:12-13 shows. According to 1 Corinthians 12:3, the contrast to "Jesus is Lord" is "Jesus be cursed." Thus, the acclamation of his lordship is that of the believing church, as opposed to its rejection by others. Romans 1:4, to which I shall turn presently, sees his status after the resurrection in terms of a Davidic kingship over God's people. Second, the belief in the God who raised Jesus from the dead leads to salvation, namely, as the future tense of the verb shows, in the last judgment.[1]

The same is true for 1 Thessalonians 1:9-10, a summary of Paul's missionary preaching, which had made the Thessalonians "turn to God from idols to serve a living and true God and to wait for his Son from heaven, whom he raised from the dead, Jesus who delivers us from the wrath to come." Again, belief in the God who raised Jesus will bring salvation at his parousia.

---

[1]Romans 10:10 does not say that the believer has already been justified and the confessor saved, but that believing leads to justification (as God accepts it now and/or will accept it in the last judgment) and confessing to salvation (which is, in Paul, almost exclusively the coming eternal bliss). It may be better to speak of "homologies" to avoid a misunderstanding of "creed" or "creedal formula" (as if it were an already fixed dogma accepted by the authority of the church); cf. Hulitt Gloer, "Hymns and Homologies in the New Testament," *Perspectives in Religious Studies* 11 (1984): 115-32.

Finally, the old Aramaic call *maranatha*, "Our Lord, come"[2] (1 Cor 16:22, Rev 22:20; a more probable rendering than the linguistically possible "Our Lord has come") combines the position of Jesus as Lord with his coming. Even so, we are not sure what coming is meant. In all three instances, 1 Corinthians 16:22, Didache 10:6 and (in Greek translation) Revelation 22:20, this call follows a sentence that excludes the sinner or the nonbeliever from the community of saints. It may be, therefore, that the first Christians thought of the Lord as one who comes into the assembly to judge the sinner who would not repent. Even so, it would, in their understanding, be an anticipation of his final coming. Moreover, *maranatha* is, in Didache 10:6, part of the liturgy of the eucharist, and the same life-setting has been suggested for 1 Corinthians 16:22.[3] The images of the tree of life and the holy city in Revelation 22:19 may also be influenced by eucharistic phrases. In the eucharistic passages in 1 Corinthians 10:21, 11:20, 26-27 the title "Lord" appears several times in an otherwise unusual context, combined with Jesus' blood and death, bread and cup, supper and table. This proves that the title "Lord" is rooted in the celebration of the eucharist, for which the call *maranatha* seems to have been typical, so that the Aramaic concept of *mare* ("Lord") became an element of the eucharistic celebration even prior to the later influence from the Septuagint and the Hellenistic cults.[4] Thus, belief in the resurrection of Jesus is the basis of the present status of the believer under the Lordship of Christ and of his hope for final salvation after the parousia. It attributes this to God's act on Easter day.

How far the expectation of the coming Christ shaped the life of the early church is uncertain. While some interpreters consider apocalypticism the "mother of theology"[5] or at least its "midwife,"[6] others deny any evidence of

---

[2]Joseph A. Fitzmyer, "The Aramaic Language and the Study of the New Testament," *Journal of Biblical Literature* 99 (1980): 13-14; Fitzmyer, *To Advance the Gospel* (New York: Crossroads, 1981) 228-29.

[3]Günther Bornkamm, *Das Ende des Gesetzes* (Munich: Kaiser, 1952) 123-32; against Bornkamm, J. D. G. Dunn, *Unity and Diversity in the New Testament* (London: SCM Press, 1977) 55.

[4]Eduard Schweizer, *Erniedrigung und Erhöhung bei Jesus und seinen Nachfolgern*, Abhandlungen zur Theologie des Alten und Neuen Testaments 28 (Zurich: Zwingli Verlag, 1962) 80-83 with notes 325a-f; see also Schweizer, *Jesus* (London: SCM, 1971) 56n7, 67n4.

[5]Ernst Käsemann, "Zum Thema der urchristlichen Apokalyptik," in *Exegetische Versuche und Besinnungen*, 2 vols. (Göttingen: Vandenhoeck und Ruprecht, 1964) 2:130.

[6]Eduard Schweizer, "I Kor 15, 20-28 als Zeugnis paulinischer Eschatologie und ihrer Verwandtschaft mit der Verkündigung Jesu," in *Jesus und Paulus* [Festschrift für W. G. Kümmel], ed. E. Earle Ellis and Erich Grässer (Göttingen: Vandenhoeck und Ruprecht, 1975) 314. An English version of this essay appeared in *Saved by Grace* [Festschrift for R. C. Oudersluys], ed. James I. Cook (Grand Rapids: William B. Eerdmans, 1978) 132.

a dominating apocalyptic tendency in the period under consideration.[7] The proclamation of an imminent parousia, of the judgment, and of the kingdom of God is to be found in John the Baptist (Mt 3:10-12), in some words of Jesus (which may have been created by the church, Mk 9:1, 13:30), in Paul's earliest letter (1 Thess 4:17), in Revelation (1:1, 22:20) and in the Didache (16). Jesus started his ministry from the baptism by John; he gave up his fasting and baptizing, but not his proclamation of the coming kingdom, though he also spoke of its presence and never gave any details or helps to calculate the date of its arrival. It is difficult to think that the hope for an imminent coming of the kingdom did not influence the earliest church to a considerable degree. Furthermore, in Acts (11:27-28; 15:32; 21:8, 10; also 13:1) Luke mentions prophets coming from Jerusalem (or, at least, Palestine), though he reports nothing of their activity there, since the apostles (not the sometimes unreliable prophets) are, for him, the sound basis of the church. Itinerant prophets also played some role in Matthew's church and in the church of the Didache, and continued to function up to the fourth century when the monastic movement took up their impetus. Note, however, that the parousia or the coming kingdom are never mentioned in a creedal formula. The same may be said of the belief in one God. Both the belief in one God and the parousia or the coming kingdom are presupposed and explicitly mentioned only in the preaching to the Gentiles (1 Thess 1:9-10). And yet, without this assumed basis, faith would be senseless.

In Romans 1:3-4 Paul quotes a creed, probably of Jewish-Christian origin and known to the Roman Church. In it Jesus is portrayed as the promised son of David who ascended to his throne and became the son of God in power by his resurrection, like the Israelite king who became, according to Psalm 2:7, son of God. Unlike the Israelite king, however, Jesus has become the Son of God definitively and forever, fulfilling the promise of God given to David. He was already in his earthly ministry ("according to the flesh") the promised Davidic messiah who began to rule over the people of God "according to the Holy Spirit" on Easter day. His human existence was a preliminary stage in which he was the designated, but not yet ruling king. Again, resurrection is installation to lordship over the church. The future dimension is not mentioned, but the link with the Old Testament is introduced by the reference to Jesus' descent from David.[8]

---

[7]Günter Klein, "Eschatologie," *Theologische Realenzyklopädie* (Berlin: Walter de Gruyter, 1976) 10:274-75.

[8]Whether "according to the flesh" and "according to the Spirit of holiness" (thus, literally) belong to the original creed (as I think) or are Pauline additions is still discussed. The latter is possible, because this contrast is, in the New Testament, not to be found outside of the Pauline letters and writings dependent on them; the former is, perhaps, plausible because this is an Old Testament contrast (Isa 31:3; cf. Num 16:22, 27:16 LXX; 1QM 7:5; 1QH 9:16) and Paul never uses "according to the flesh" in a neutral sense when set in opposition to "according to the Spirit" or even when used alone combined with a verb (not with a noun). Cf. Eduard Schweizer, "Röm. 1. 3f. und der Gegensatz von Fleisch und Geist vor und bei Paulus," *Evangelische Theologie* 15 (1955): 563-71.

(b) " . . . for our sake"

No creed speaks of God's act in an abstract way, separated from what this act accomplishes in the lives of believers. With the exception of the summary of Paul's missionary preaching, however, the notion that they have become the people of the Lord or God's redeemed people is only implied in the formulae mentioned above. The proper place to introduce the "we" of the confessing church is the crucifixion of Jesus. Even the short phrase in 1 Thessalonians 5:10 contains this "we": "our Lord Jesus Christ who died for our sake." Romans 3:25 expands this short statement in traditional language with a reference to the Old Testament expiation on the cover of the mercy seat (Lev 16:13-15). In a similar way Romans 4:25 ("Jesus our Lord, who was delivered up because of our transgressions") includes the effect on the believer and echoes Isaiah 53:5-6, 12 (compare the introduction to the eucharist as recorded by Paul in 1 Cor 11:23: "The Lord Jesus, on the night in which he was delivered up," and Paul's own variant in Gal 2:20, "The son of God delivered himself up for my sake").[9] Such an interpretation shows the influence of the sacrificial death of the victim,[10] although this is not the only possible interpretation. The mere "for our sake" can express any form of representation. The term "ransom" points to the idea of liberation from slavery. The concept of participation in the death of Christ ("one has died for all, thus all have died," 2 Cor 5:14) presupposes an inclusion in the destiny of Christ. The pattern in the sermons in Acts ("Jesus whom you have crucified, God has raised" etc.) sees his death as the graceful opportunity to convert and find salvation just by confessing one's sin. But the image of the sacrifice stresses the absolute priority of God's act over against all our work, even our gratitude or faith, as does no other imagery.

Very early, Jesus' death and resurrection were combined: "we believe that Jesus died and rose" (1 Thess 4:14). This is traditional language, typical of the Synoptics and Acts, but not of Paul, who uses another verb and puts it in the passive voice ("being raised"). In 1 Corinthians 15:3-5 Paul quotes a creed that he had received (in Jerusalem? in Antioch?) and handed down to the churches he had founded. It is constructed in a remarkably parallel way. Two principal statements "he died" and "he has been raised" are followed by two facts that confirm them: "he was buried" and "he was seen by Cephas and the twelve." His death is interpreted by the phrase "for our sins," his resurrection by "on the third day," and both are said to have happened "according to the scriptures." Thus, the "we" of the confessors appears when the effect of the death of Jesus is mentioned. This is emphasized because it transformed the situation of the believers, separated from God and threatened by his wrath, to that of

---

[9]Wiard Popkes, *Christus Traditus*, Abhandlungen zur Theologie des Alten und Neuen Testaments 49 (Zurich: Zwingli Verlag, 1967) esp. 251-70.

[10]Cf. Peter Stuhlmacher, "Sühne oder Versöhnung?" in *Die Mitte des Neuen Testaments* [Festschrift für E. Schweizer] (Göttingen: Vandenhoeck und Ruprecht, 1983) 291-316, esp. 300-304.

the new people of God. The continuity of Old and New Testament is seen as an avenue that leads from promise to fulfillment (as in Rom 1:3, "born from Davidic descent").

The resurrection is seen as installation to lordship over the church (as in Rom 1:4), for, unlike the other verbs, "raised" is a Greek perfect that emphasizes that what has happened in the past (the resurrection itself) is continuing to influence the present (Jesus is ruling as the risen one). The implication of the coming judgment is clear ("for our sins"). Hence, we are still in a church that shares some main characteristics with Israel. (1) It is thinking in terms of time that moves from an origin in the past (be it the election of Abraham, the deliverance from Egypt or, as here, the prophetic promises) through the present (understood as the freedom of the saved children of God, here under the lordship of Christ) to a final goal (the everlasting life with God from whom no sin separates us anymore). (2) The main obstacle on this road is sin—man's opposition to God's will by deeds, words or thoughts—and nobody can remove this obstacle except God himself. Basically, this creed must go back to the time of Paul's first visit in Jerusalem, no later than five years after Jesus' death. It was preached by him in Corinth "as of first importance" or "in the very beginning" (both translations are possible).[11] It shows that from the beginning the experience of the Lordship of the risen Christ was for the church "good news," because the death of Jesus on the cross, interpreted in different ways, brought about the new relation of God to mankind. This safeguarded the initiative of God in his act "outside of us" and "before us."[12]

Finally, a fixed phrase, though not a creedal formula in the strict sense, says that "God sent his son in order to. . . . " We find it in Paul (Gal 4:4, Rom 8:3) and in John (3:16-17, 1 John 4:9).[13] It is surprising that the goal introduced by "in order that" is always salvation in the death of Jesus. In Galatians 4:5 the phrase "to redeem those who were under the law" repeats the statement of Galatians 3:13, "Christ redeemed us from the curse of the law, having

---

[11]The formulation of the creed is, word by word, un-Pauline, which shows that Paul received it in an already fixed form either in Antioch or in Jerusalem. At any rate, it could not have been basically different from what Paul learned in Jerusalem during the two weeks that he stayed there about two or three years after having been called to his apostleship.

[12]This is my main objection to Daniel Patte's important and provocative book *Paul's Faith and the Power of the Gospel* (Philadelphia: Fortress, 1983), which understands the experience of Jesus as a creative exemple for that of the apostle, which in its course becomes the same for the believer.

[13]It is always "God," not "the Father" or "the Lord" or any other title; the verb for "sending" may vary though the meaning is always the same; then again, "his son" is always the object, and a sentence introduced by "in order to" indicates the goal of this sending. John 3:16 reads "God gave (his, p⁶³ and other witnesses) son"; 14:16-26 ("the Father will give/will send the paraclete"), shows, however, that "to give" and "to send" are synonymous in John.

become a curse for us; for it is written,[14] 'Cursed be everyone who hangs on a tree' [the cross].'' In Romans 8:3 the expression "for sin" means, as in Leviticus 5:7 and almost 20 other passages, "as a sin offering." In John 3:16 the final clause repeats literally (with one addition) the final clause of the preceding verse, which speaks of the Son of man exalted (to the cross) like the serpent in the desert (Num 21:8-9), and the "sending of his (God's) son" in 1 John 4:9 is interpreted in the following verse by "expiation for our sins." Thus, the coming into the world of the one who is God's son before his incarnation is combined in all four passages—therefore probably traditionally—with Jesus' death on the cross.

An examination of these creedal formulae suggests the following conclusions. (1) The subject of all the verbs (except those in the fixed phrase just mentioned) is Jesus Christ, but not God or the Holy Spirit or the believer with his or her conversion. (2) All the verbs appear in the passive voice except "he died," which is, in and of itself, a passive occurrence. Thus, these formulae all understand Jesus as the object of God's acts. (3) The core of these creeds is, either Jesus resurrection to lordship over the church, or Jesus death for our sins. Very early—implicitly from the very beginning—this is seen as fulfillment of Old Testament promises. Both cores are paralleled and interpreted as early as in the creed that Paul received. (4) No creed speaks of the earthly ministry of Jesus. It is always the borderlines between earthly and heavenly existence that are mentioned: cross and resurrection and occasionally his birth; that is, the events that indicate that the status of Jesus transcends that of any other human being, a status often understood as the fulfillment of the promise to David or of the Scriptures in general or as the result of a sending act of God. (5) The parousia is not mentioned explicitly (except in preaching to Gentiles), though it is presupposed, since the expectation of a final judgment is implied in phrases like "for our sins." The preexistence of Christ with God is not mentioned either, but the phrase "God sending his Son" or the focus on Christ as the mediator of the first and the second creation (1 Cor. 8:6) show, as well as the hymns to which we shall turn in a moment, that this idea, analogous to that of Wisdom or Logos, lies in the background of some early Christian confessions. (6) The effect on the believer is primarily combined wth Jesus' death (Paul emphasizes the death on the *cross*) though his present Lordship is effected by his resurrection.

(c) The Christology of Early Christian Hymns

What is a hymn? For a long time scholars distinguished the "Hellenistic" hymns from the "Jewish" creeds. Recently, however, Martin Hengel[15] and others have shown how much Hellenism had already influenced Palestinian Judaism beginning as early as the middle of the third century B.C., the begin-

---

[14]Deut 21:23, also in 11Q Temple 64:12.

[15]Martin Hengel, "Judentum and Hellenismus," *Wissenschaftliche Untersuchungen zum Neuen Testament* 10 (1973): esp. 8-107, 108-95; quotation on 193.

ning of "Hellenistic Judaism in the strict sense." We come nearer to under-standing the nature of a hymn when we realize how different the language of a creed is from that of a hymn. In a creed, we are speaking to our fellowmen, bearing witness of our faith in order to invite others to faith or to confirm oth-ers in the same faith. In a hymn, we are already one with all the believers who sing with us, addressing the exalted lord; thus, our common faith is the basis of our act. It is not something we have to convey to others and to adapt to the situation of the hearers. When the prodigal son was overwhelmed by the love of his father, he could have fallen down exclaiming (in a "hymnic" way), "Fa-ther, your love is unbelievable; there is nothing indeed that you would not for-give," and this outburst would be the appropriate fitting praise of this love. But suppose he were speaking to a younger brother who wanted to go the same way he had once gone, seeing and enjoying the world and its good life. In this situation he might say, "You know, the love of the father is unbelievable, there is nothing indeed that he would not forgive," but apart from the context of thanking his father, the same sentence would express exactly the opposite of what it meant when spoken in gratitude and praise. Even an additional warn-ing of the younger brother against abuse—"Of course, you are to come back as a humble and contrite sinner, as I did"—would change nothing. There is a language of praise that simply cannot be used meaningfully outside of the ex-perience granted to the speaker. It is impossible to anticipate the experience of a forgiving father in the advice to the younger brother, because by doing so, we should deprive the giver of his freedom to love. Thus, language of praise cannot become directly the language of doctrine, which informs the believer or the unbeliever about a truth in the form of a continually valid definition. Since a hymn is sung in gratitude to and in praise of the exalted Christ and addressed to him alone, it is not necessary to explain to him who he is and who he is not, to offer him a total picture of his importance or to fight against pos-sible misunderstandings. Nor is it necessary to describe the faith of the singers, either defining it in a comprehensive way or protecting it from deterioration. Thus, a psalm like Psalm 103 praises the one who "forgives *all* your iniquities, who heals *all* your diseases," and is sung by someone who has experienced this; it is not a doctrinal statement that assures anyone in or outside Israel that this will always happen. Israel is so aware of the freedom of its God, "I shall be who I shall be" (never at the disposal of the believer), that it does not even dare to pronounce the name of God lest it offend against his freedom by encasing him in a definition, a title or a name, which would set limits to that freedom. It may have been easier for a Gentile or Jewish Hellenist to overcome this barrier. Ec-stasy, in which he or she transcended the limits of earthly existence and be-came in some way one with God, may have been more familiar to them than to a typical Palestinian apocalypticist who, even in his visions, always experi-enced his distance from God. Be this as it may, the language of the hymn is, by necessity, different from that of a creedal or even a doctrinal statement.

(d) The Hymns in the New Testament

Philippians 2:6-11, perhaps the earliest of the New Testament hymns, fo-cuses initially on the heavenly position of the one adored in this song. No name or title is given, only the relative pronoun "who" at the beginning, since the singing community knows *who* this is. The act of becoming man is described as "emptying himself" of the status (or the form) of God and is then interpreted as humiliation and obedience "in the likeness of man" leading to his death. Whether the addition "even death on the cross" belongs to the original hymn or is added by Paul is disputed. There follows the exaltation and the bestowing of a name on him, at which angels and men and demons will bow, confessing that Jesus Christ is Lord. The most significant question raised by this affirmation is whether this bowing and confessing described in verses 10-11 is thought of as already happening, as passages like 1 Timothy 3:16 or Colossians 2:15 might suggest, or as a future event at the parousia. Paul must have understood it in the latter way, if he had not changed his theology,[16] since he quoted the same Old Testament verse in Romans 14:11 as pointing to God's last judgment and since he wrote in 1 Corinthians 15:24-27 that the last enemy, death, will be subjected only at the parousia. Even with regard to the original hymn, much can be said for this interpretation, because the closest parallels are Old Testament hymns praising the eschatological theophany.[17]

If, however, it were understood originally as being true already and always, could this hymn be seen as a pre-Pauline witness to the existence of the Gnostic pattern of a descent and ascent of the saviour? We cannot exclude this possibility, though it is, in my view, improbable.[18] First, the term of self-humiliation is only used in a spiritual sense in Paul's time and is not identical with "descending." Second, we do not hear of an ascent in this text, but of an exaltation granted by God in response to obedience. Both ideas are totally alien to Gnosticism. There is, however, an even more important reason for rejecting a Gnostic origin for this hymn. The idea of Jesus exalted to heaven has its origin in the post-Easter experiences of the disciples and has been developed along the lines of the Jewish expectation of a "resurrection of the dead"[19] at the end of time. Psalm 110:1 ("The Lord says to my lord: sit at my right hand") has also influenced this idea, and perhaps also the heavenly journeys narrated in the visions of the Jewish apocalypticists. A kind of "descent" of the Son has been developed independently along the lines of the sending of prophets and angels by God, and the picture of the Wisdom of God, having its "throne" or its "home" in heaven, "coming to look for a dwelling among men" (Eth. Enoch 42:1-2, similarly Ben Sirach 24:4-7) has again influenced this idea, without any connection with a later ascent. Conversely, the exaltation of Christ is widely

---

[16]As G. B. Caird, *Principalities and Powers* (Oxford: Clarendon Press, 1956) 27-28 thought he did. Cf. also Heb 10:13 for the same view as in 1 Cor 15:24-27.

[17]Thus Otfried Hofius, *Der Christushymnus Phil. 2, 6-11*, Wissenschaftliche Untersuchungen zum Neuen Testament 17 (1976) 41-55.

[18]Cf. Eduard Schweizer, "Paul's Christology and Gnosticism" in *Paul and Paulinism* [Festschrift for C. K. Barrett], ed. M. D. Hooker and S. G. Wilson (London: SPCK, 1982) 119-22.

[19]"Resurrection of the dead" even with regard to Jesus' resurrection in Rom 1:4.

mentioned in the New Testament without being combined with his coming from or being sent by God, let alone with his descending from heaven. Also, the concept of preexistence in the world of God appears often, with no mention of his exaltation, let alone an ascent or a descent (1 Cor 8:6, 10:4; Col 1:15-17; cf. Gal 4:4 etc; Jn 1:1-18). Philippians 2:6-11 is the only place in the New Testament where self-humiliation (not descent) and exaltation by God (not ascent) are combined. If a Gnostic pattern were in the background (which I consider highly improbable) it would show how much Gnostic language had been transformed to express a very different message. Neither slave-like obedience with death at its climax nor a reward from God exalting the obedient servant would fit in a Gnostic scheme.

In the New Testament hymns, as in the creeds, the events that transcend a normal human life are central. Christ's former position in God's world is explicitly mentioned and emphasized and the description of his position after his exaltation is expanded. It is no longer the church alone that adores him; he is Lord not only over angels and all nations, but even over "those under the earth." Therefore, the whole universe including all those who oppose God's reign will (or even do) adore him. If this is a description of the parousia, the Jewish time factor plays a role. For the first time Jesus' earthly ministry becomes visible, though only theoretically, as a prolonging of his self-humiliation that begins in heaven and ends in his death and exaltation. It is understood in terms of obedience to God's will and framed by Christ's position in heaven at the beginning and at the end. The conviction of a final reconciliation of the whole universe is the main source of this hymn, though the description of the self-humiliation and of the obedience that lead to it suggests that believers will share this kind of life with the Christ who enables them to do so.

The most typical of the New Testament hymns is probably to be found in 1 Timothy 3:16, a text which is constructed in an artful way. Three times, an event on earth is paralleled to one in heaven, intertwined in the sequence a-b/b-a/a-b, as is typical of proverbial poetry.[20] In this way the hymn praises

  (a) the appearance on earth
  (b) the exaltation in the Spirit
  (b) the revelation to angels
  (a) the proclamation among the nations
  (a) the faith on earth
  (b) the entry into glory

Once again the hymn does not identify its subject but begins with "who" since the addressee knows his own names and titles. The limits of time are transgressed: Christ was certainly taken up in glory before he was preached among the nations and believed in the world (so much is he the center of each sentence that the hymnic formula is rendered "he is believed," not "believed on," which would suggest that the belief is the main fact and Christ merely its goal). Limits

---

[20]For instance, Proverbs 10:1-5 five times (a) describing the wise, the righteous (twice), the diligent, the prudent, and (b) his counterpart.

of space are also transgressed: Christ reviews the heavenly hosts, receives his honors, and is glorified in heaven, while he is on his way to all the nations on earth and praised by their faith. Both parades are one and the same movement for, in the presence of God, there is no time any more (Rev 10:6) nor a heavenly space separated from an earthly one (Rev 4:1). Whether this is consciously understood as anticipation of a future fulfillment or not, the emphasis lies on the totality of salvation that Christ has won and that faith experiences already in the present. All this is not proclaimed in terms of sin and judgment, but of separation and reunion. This is the language of people who have experienced the world as a heavenless and Godless place, in which heaven has become a mere sky, a brazen vault, from which all prayers and cries of men rebound, as it is described in some Hellenistic writings. It is the language of that Hellenistic world for which "Destiny" has become the highest goddess. Here, Christ is basically a heavenly, divine person. The miracle is his appearance on earth and his revelation to the believing nations.

The hymn in Colossians 1:15-20, again introduced by the relative pronoun "who," parallels the firstborn of all creation, through whom, in whom and to whom all things on earth and in heaven have been created, with the firstborn from the dead in whom, through whom and to whom the fullness of God reconciled all things on earth and in heaven. He is called "the image of the invisible God." This, however, does not refer to the earthly Jesus (who is not mentioned in this hymn except by the phrase "from the dead"), but to the preexistent mediator of the creation. This becomes understandable when we see that Philo compares the Logos of God to a coining die that represents God's power and authority so that all the coins are stamped by that authority. In this simile, "image" is not something static, but very dynamic, creating new coins after the image of God which is engraved on the coining die. The other focus is the resurrection of Christ, again understood as the "beginning" of a long line of followers. Both terms, "image" and "beginning," are also paralleled in Philo. The first stanza proclaims that all things, "visible and invisible" and "thrones, dominions, principalities, authorities" are held together by Christ; the second stanza speaks of their reconciliation in Christ, a reconciliation that has taken place in his resurrection.

Most scholars agree that the author of the letter has added his own interpretation to this hymn at two points. First, he has inserted a reference to Jesus' death on the cross in verse 20. The awkward repetition of "through him" after the insertion still shows that correction. Second, in verse 18 Christ is called "the head of the body," which the author of the letter reinterpreted by adding "namely of the church." Originally, "the head of the body" meant the head of the universe, as Greek parallels show, in which the highest God is called the head of the body, namely of the cosmos. In Philo's writings, heaven and, if the text is correctly copied, also the Logos of God are the head of the cosmic body, and the Logos is the place in which the whole cosmos is living like the blueprint of an edifice to be built in the mind of the architect.[21] That is why the text does not say "his body" or "the body of Christ," but simply, as nowhere else in the New Testament, "the body," and why Christ has become "the head" in the simile, whereas in 1 Corinthians 12, the head is simply one member among others.

Thus, a very interesting development has taken place. Again Christ is the preexistent mediator of creation, God's coining die, and the risen Lord, in whom the fullness of God reconciles the universe. Again the earthly ministry of Jesus plays no role, even the cross was originally not mentioned, though his death is implied in the phrase "from the dead," but only as a kind of gateway to the exaltation. The new tune in this hymn is its universalistic outlook. Certainly the church is the group of those who already know the savior and, therefore, can sing this hymn full of joy and thanksgiving, but reconciliation reaches beyond the limits of the church and has already embraced the whole creation. Through the resurrection of Jesus Christ heaven and earth have, objectively, been united again, so that the new creation is already reality. This is, perhaps, the most "hymnic hymn" because it obviously anticipates what is not yet to be seen. The first stanza declares that the whole creation is living in Christ, held together by him; the second states that it is reconciled by him, without any indication that a break has happened in between. Why did Christ have to die and to be raised if everything is living in him? There is no answer because a hymn is not a creed or a doctrinal statement. A hymn addresses the risen Christ without concern for possible misunderstandings. It is sung face to face to the exalted Lord and praises him for what he is. What is he? He is both the creator and the reconciler. Therefore, as long as the singing church is looking exclusively to him, it is true that he is the power of all creation coming into being, and the power of all creation being brought back in reconciliation to God.

Perhaps the best known of the New Testament hymns is the prologue to the Fourth Gospel. Here, too, we have to distinguish between the original hymn and some additional interpretation. John 1:6-8 suddenly speaks of John the Baptist, who becomes, grammatically, the subject, whereas in verse 9, the subject is again, without any indication of the change, the Logos as in verses 1-5. The one who inserted the reference to John the Baptist must have understood the following verses to be a description of Jesus, the incarnate Logos, baptized by John. In this case, verse 14 ("And the Logos became flesh") would no longer be the climax, but rather a summarizing repetition of what verses 9-13 had already stated. Similarly, verses 15, and, perhaps, 17 seem to have been added by a redactor. However, all the details of the structure of the original hymn are debatable: whether it was a Jewish text that spoke of the Logos, the Word of God, dwelling in the world and granting to the Israelites the right to become children of God lies in the background (verses 1, 3-4, 9-12b);[22] whether there

[21]Eduard Schweizer, "σῶμα," *Theological Dictionary of the New Testament*, 10 vols., ed. Gerhard Friedrich, trans. Geoffrey W. Bromiley (Grand Rapids: William B. Eerdmans, 1971) 7:1036, 1054-55.

[22]U. B. Müller, *Die Geschichte der Christologie in der johanneischen Gemeinde*, Stuttgarter Bibelstudien 77 (1975) 13-47.

are two or even three[23] different layers to be seen; and whether the famous climax of "the Word became flesh" might not be a later correction made by the church after the evangelist had completed his book.[24] Regardless of one's conclusions in these matters, it is indisputable that this prologue, with or without any additions, was and is, as soon as it ran beyond verse 12b, a Christian hymn praising the preexistent and the incarnate Word of God. Like Colossians 1:15-20, it emphasizes his activity in the creation. Even more than in Colossians, the language of Jewish wisdom-texts dominates the first part of the hymn.[25] Beyond what is also said in Colossians 1, John 1:11-12 tells about the rejection of this Word of God by the world into which it came, and of its reception by some who became children of God. In the original hymn, this probably refers to the Israelites or to a group among them who opened themselves to the Wisdom of God. In the understanding of the evangelist, however, this refers to the Christians. The second part of the hymn speaks of the incarnation of the Word, not of the resurrection or exaltation of Christ. This is the more interesting, because, according to John 1:14, it is incarnation that offers the glimpse of the divine glory, which resurrection and exaltation offer according to the other hymns. Actually verse 18 suggests that even the incarnate Christ is still living in the bosom of the Father, even being the "only begotten God" (as John probably wrote[26]). Thus, final glory has already been revealed in the earthly Jesus, who is, therefore, the climax of God's revelation.

When we look back at these early creeds and hymns, the answers to the question "Who is Jesus Christ?" are very different. And yet they all have something in common. They are not interested in his earthly ministry, but rather in the events that frame it and give it a character of transcendence. Jesus transcends any other human being as the one who was living with God before becoming man, who suffered a death that was itself transcended, since it is still present for those that share it and are saved by it, and who was raised from the dead to a lordship over church and world which will lead to the final salvation at his parousia. Of course, not all these elements are mentioned or implied in any one text.

---

[23]Thus, for instance, John Painter, "Christology and the History of the Johannine Community in the Fourth Gospel," *New Testament Studies* 30 (1984): 460-74.

[24]Georg Richter, *Studien zum Johannesevangelium*, Biblische Untersuchungen 13 (1979) 169, 196-98. This is difficult to believe because, in this case, there would be no real climax in the hymn.

[25]Long ago, C. H. Dodd collected quite a number of literal parallels. See *The Interpretation of the Fourth Gospel* (Cambridge: Cambridge University Press, 1953) 274-77.

[26]All important manuscripts read "God." The easier reading "Son" is probably a later correction to avoid the difficulty; it may have been caused by the change of only one letter, which would have transformed "the only begotten God" into "the only begotten of God."

(e) Paul

Most of these creeds and even hymns predate Paul's letters and while some may have been created later, they represent, by and large, the faith that he found in the church. His importance lies in the way in which he brought together all these approaches and focused them in his understanding of crucifixion and resurrection. When, in Romans 5:12-21, he draws a picture of the history of God with mankind, he makes a very surprising statement in verse 20: "Law came in to increase sin, but when sin had reached its climax, grace abounded all the more." Thus, sin reaches its climax exactly where the law of God rules, and this is the distinctive mark of Israel. All nations know about deeds that are wrong: murder, robbery, adultery, and so on. But the perception persists of a kind of existence in which people do not murder, rob or commit adultery and are, therefore, free of sin. It is only the law of God, given to Israel, that showed Israel and through Israel all nations that there is no existence that is free from sin. In fact, the very ones who thought they had kept all the commandments "did do what they did not want to" (Rom 7:16) and brought sin to its climax, because they "boast"[27] that they were not sinners like the Gentiles. This is what Paul had experienced himself. He was so eager to fulfill the law that he even persecuted those who, in his view, opposed it, until he realized near Damascus that he had, in his piety, sidestepped God.

This is demonstrated clearly in the ministry and the crucifixion of Jesus. During his ministry, it became more and more clear that many rejected him, but there were still others who did not fight against him and were even enthusiastic about him. Twelve men and a group of women stayed close to him even when it became dangerous to do so. And then, one of them betrayed him, one denied knowing him, all the men fled, and the women stood at the cross looking from far away. No one was present to fulfill the most important duty of burying him except an outsider (perhaps a partial believer). Sin came to its climax, for it was not only murderers or prostitutes who failed to see God acting in this death, but even his closest friends who had left everything to follow him. Yet grace abounded. It was to these very people that the risen Lord appeared, and it was Paul that he called to become his most important apostle. The death of Jesus was necessary to show that there is no one who can live without the grace of God, and the resurrection was necessary to show that there is no one whom God's grace cannot heal. Round this mystery of cross and resurrection Paul is always circling. He can express it in many ways as the church did before him.[28] It is clear, however, that the truth, the whole truth of his proclamation, depends on the reality of God's unique presence in Jesus, which fulfilled all his promises. Paul certainly knew about the earthly ministry of Jesus—he presupposes knowledge of the last days in Jerusalem (1 Cor 11:23), of Jesus' pov-

---

[27]The root of this word ($\varkappa\alpha\upsilon\chi$-) appears frequently in all the undisputed letters of Paul except the very short one to Philemon.

[28]Cf. the beginning of §b in this chapter.

erty (2 Cor 8:9), of his Jewish, even Davidic descent (Rom 9:5, 1:3), of some sayings like 1 Corinthians 7:10, whereas in the letters of John we find not a single hint of this earthly ministry (except perhaps 1 Jn 1:1-3), though their author must know the gospel. Still, for Paul, the one decisive fact was the presence of God in the death and the resurrection of Jesus, because there would be no salvation if it had not been God himself who acted for our sake. A harmless Jesus, a mere teacher and moral example or even a prophet, would not help us.

In a similar way, John takes up creeds and hymns of the church. In the next chapter I shall show that, while John's language may be very different from that of Paul, his understanding of Jesus as the only one who can give us real life is very similar to Paul's. The contrast is not confined to human righteousness or wisdom over against justification by God's righteousness and wisdom as in Paul. In John it is put into a more universal form: it is the contrast between anything on which a person may base his or her own life and God's saving presence in Jesus Christ. Thus, even John, though writing a gospel, starts from the insight of the post-Easter church that it is God himself who encounters us in Jesus Christ, who came from God and was exalted again to oneness with God, opening the way to the Father to all his followers.

Chapter 3

NARRATIVE ANSWERS IN THE NEW TESTAMENT

(a) Q—A Source Containing Sayings of Jesus

I have shown in the last chapter that there was no formula or hymn, let alone theological system (like that of Paul or John), in which the kerygma was not rooted in the soil of history. While this may have been reduced to a statement about the appearance "in the flesh" (1 Tim 3:16) or to a phrase about the "firstborn from the dead" (Col 1:18), there is no proclamation of God's Christ without a reference to the human person of Jesus. If one isolated these from their context and confused a hymn of praise with a creedal statement, then the danger of a *docetic Christology*, in which Jesus of Nazareth is seen as a mere symbol or example, would be a real threat. The same could happen if Paul's references to the crucified Jesus were misunderstood as mere illustrations of a timeless truth, namely, of the fact that victory may be hidden in apparent failure, strength in weakness. Then Paul's proclamation of Jesus Christ would be reduced to the insight that man often learns in outward defeat to trust in his innermost, divine self and to understand his existence not as something he can dispose of but as something given to him. The myth of a Hellenistic god like Attis, who had, according to the legend, died and risen again, would serve equally well to illustrate such a truth. This is what has happened to the Christian message in Gnosticism. For Paul, the death of Jesus on the cross was such a scandal that he would never forget how shockingly historical it was; for the churches in Greece, it was an event in a faraway corner of the Empire, receding more and more into the obscurity of the past. Thus, it became urgent to tell the story of Jesus in its historical context. If, conversely, one ever forgot that it was the story of the one whom God had raised from the dead, an *Ebionite Christology* would arise, in which Jesus would be nothing but a teacher and example, perhaps the greatest of all men, but still not more than a man.

Is such an Ebionite Christology to be found in the New Testament? This is what some scholars suggest. Their starting point is the two-source hypothesis, which suggests that Matthew and Luke knew Mark and another source from which the material common to both of them was drawn. This source (lacking in Mark) has been designated Q (from the German *Quelle*, "source") and contains mostly sayings of Jesus. It has been suggested that Q was used in a church in which Jesus was perceived as a prophetic teacher who emphasized an ethical conversion in view of the near coming of the kingdom of God and the judgment by the Son of man. In its earlier layers, Q would not have contained Christological titles like Son of God nor the identification of the Son of man with Jesus. It would have been a collection of ethical directions, originating in Galilee, whereas the church in Jerusalem concentrated its preaching on the death and resurrection of Jesus. Some scholars would add a pre-Markan source in which Jesus was a miracle worker, a pre-Johannine one in which he was the prophetic messenger sent by God, and a pre-Pauline one in which he was a kind of a Gnostic saviour descending from heaven and ascending again.[1] Even so, the decisive difference with the Christology of the crucified and risen Christ would be the perception of Jesus as a mere human being, a prophetic teacher of ethics. The existence of such a group would raise the possibility that the church grew out of at least two groups of followers of Jesus with very different Christological patterns, one located in Galilee, the other in Jerusalem.[2]

I grant to these scholars that the two-source hypothesis, according to which Q existed as a written document[3] beside Mark, is still the most probable solution of the Synoptic problem. Thus, let us first look at Q, and then discuss whether a two-root hypothesis is a probable approach to the history of the earliest church.

Q certainly begins with the words of John the Baptist about the One to come who would be greater than John himself, and with the temptation story, in which the divine sonship of Jesus is presupposed (probably because his baptism was also recounted). It contains Jesus' prayer to the Father who knows the Son (Lk 10:21-22) and the conviction of Jesus to be the One to come (by whom the blind receive their sight, the lame walk, lepers are cleansed and the deaf hear, the dead are raised up and the poor have good news preached to them, Lk 7:22). Even if this were a late development within Q (though clear criteria for distinguishing different layers are still missing), the difference between this and a collection of wise words is evident. Jesus is the one in whom the final

---

[1]S. Schulz, *Q—die Spruchquelle der Evangelisten* (Zurich: Theologischer Verlag, 1972) 31, 486-87, cf. n. 8 below.

[2]Later testimonies of a Christology that knew Jesus only as a prophet teacher and as the coming judge would include the gospel of Thomas, the Didache and, with some variations, several Gnostic writings; cf. Helmut Köster in Köster and James Robinson, *Entwicklungslinien durch die Welt des frühen Christentums* (Tübingen: J. C. B. Mohr, 1971) esp. 4/III and 5/II, also 4/II at the end.

[3]This is, at least, very probable for the first part, in which sequence and content agree: words of John the Baptist, (baptism of Jesus), temptation of Jesus, the material common to the Sermon on the Mount/Plain, the healing of the servant of the centurion in Capernaum.

climax of all history has come: why are people not able to interpret the times (Lk 12:54-59); since John the Baptist the turning of the ages has come (Lk 16:16); all the blood shed from the foundation of the world will be required of this generation (Lk 11:50-51). He, Jesus, is the Son of man (Lk 6:22; 7:34; 9:58) who will come to judge (Lk 12:35-46; 17:22-37) according to whether men have accepted or rejected him in his earthly ministry (Lk 12:8-12), and the worst sinners of the Scripture, Sodom and Gomorrah, will then be better off than the towns that have seen his deeds without repenting (Lk 10:12-15). Then he will be called "Lord, Lord," as he is already called (Lk 13:25; 6:46). In him something greater than Jonah and Solomon and even John the Baptist has come, for the kingdom of God is present in his activity (Lk 11:29-32; 7:28; 10:20). Therefore, he speaks on his own authority: "Amen, I say to you" (Lk 7:9, 28; 10:12, 24; 11:51). Prophets and kings desired to see but did not see what the disciples see now (Lk 10:24).

Even more important, the parables reported in Q are not merely illustrations of a wisdom that would be true in all times and places. There is always something very surprising in them, an element which is far from being self-evident. What lord would gird himself and serve his slaves at table (Lk 12:37)? What mustard seed grows so that it becomes a tree (Lk 13:18)? What woman would bake bread to feed a hundred persons (Lk 13:21; "hiding" the leaven in the dough is an unexpected expression to describe her activity)? What noble man would invite poor and maimed and blind and lame to a great banquet (Lk 14:15-24)? It is now in Jesus' activity that all this happens because, in it, the kingdom of God approaches men. This is precisely the reason that Jesus uses parabolic language. The traditional picture that we have of religious teaching is something like the following: On the one hand there is a teacher, a prophet or even the messiah, whose head is filled with divine knowledge (if we were pietists, it would be his heart filled with divine love; if we were Africans, it would be his belly filled with divine power). On the other hand, there are people, to whose heads or hearts or bellies this divine knowledge or love or power is transferred. This picture is not true. When Peter preaches to Cornelius (Acts 10) he learns from what God had revealed to Cornelius as much as Cornelius learns from him, and even less is this traditional picture true when we think of Jesus' teaching. Though, in his case, the stream of God's word, love and power flows from him to the hearers, Jesus knows that real communication only happens when communion is created. Therefore, he speaks in parables.

Unlike a language of (doctrinal) information, which remains outside of the hearer so that the hearer can observe and judge, accept or reject it, a parable, if understood at all, sets experiences in motion. It enters a person and starts a process of sensations. The hearer may still stop this process and reject the message of the parable, but even so, something has happened to him or her, and he or she is no longer the same as before. A parable can only be understood if it (and in it the kingdom itself) seizes us, or, as John D. Crossan has suggested, if we enter and experience it from inside.[4] In it, the kingdom of God comes,

---

[4]John D. Crossan, *In Parables* (New York: Harper and Row, 1973) 13. I owe the three pictures of religious teaching to Walter Hollenweger.

not in the form of a new information, but in the form of a new way of thinking and living.

A recognition of this appears in the Q material. Therefore, even in Q, the sayings of Jesus are, more and more, set in the context of his ministry. The Sermon on the Mount or Plain is spoken to disciples that Jesus had called and to the crowds. Jesus quotes the prophecy of Isaiah to the two disciples whom John the Baptist had sent to him out of the prison. The missionary rules are given to the disciples sent to prepare his way. The pronouncement of the presence of the kingdom of God is closely connected with the healing of a demoniac and similar events. Q even reports whole stories like that of the centurion in Capernaum or that of the temptation of Jesus though the emphasis may lie on the sayings of Jesus.

This material, however, presents no explicit Christology, and neither the cross nor the resurrection of Jesus are mentioned in Q. Yet his exaltation is doubtless presupposed in the sayings about his coming as judge or witness in the last judgment (Lk 12:8-9 etc., probably also in 10:22 "All things have been delivered to me"). His coming death is foreshadowed in his rejection (Lk 7:34; 10:12-15; 11:29-32). He is the Son of man who has nowhere to lay his head (Lk 9:58), and whoever follows him has to bear his cross (Lk 14:27). This is no theory of a sacrificial or atoning death and of a resurrection as guarantee of everlasting life, because death and resurrection are not narrated as saving facts. They are rather to be relived by his followers.[5] The emphasis is certainly different from the kerygma that we find in early formulae, in hymns and in the letters of Paul.

Was Q a document originating in another church distinct from the Jerusalem church? We cannot be sure, but certain factors suggest the rejection of such a view. What evidence suggests to us that Q was ever the only Christological basis of a church? Could it not be the case that it was read in a church that proclaimed also the crucified and risen Lord, perhaps in its liturgy of the eucharist?[6] Paul, having been called to apostleship in Damascus (where Galilean influence would be expected) not more than two or three years after Jesus' death[7] knows of only one early church (in Jerusalem), the leaders of which were all Galileans. More important, the passion story originated in Jerusalem. Even the creedal formula in 1 Corinthians 15:3-5 was a short report of facts within a historical context: death, burial, resurrection appearances, emphasizing the

---

[5]M. Sato, "Q und Prophetie" (Dissertation, University of Bern, 1984) 5.1, 8.

[6]The Didache, in some ways similar to Q, emphasizes baptism and eucharist, without, however, a concept of Jesus' sacrificial death.

[7]Gal 1:18; 2:1; Acts 18:12 (Gallio ruling A.D. 51-52 or 52-53). This could only be different if Acts 15 happened chronologically after Acts 18; so Gerd Lüdemann, *Paulus der Heidenapostel* I, Forschungen zur Religion und Literatur des Alten und Neuen Testament (1980) 125, summary 207-12. Lüdemann, however, dates the call of Paul to A.D. 30[-33]. The incident with Gallio would have happened on Paul's second or third visit in Corinth (see 197).

"marginal" events of the earthly life of Jesus, and defining this life as that of the Christ of God. The confession "he died for our sins" was expanded very early, in a tradition that came to both Mark and John, as a story told in words borrowed from the psalms of the suffering righteous. Thus, narratives were also at home in the Jerusalem church. The passion report also included apolcalyptic and prophetic sayings of Jesus (the word against the temple, the warning of Judas and Peter, the prophecy of the march to Galilee), liturgical tradition (the last supper), parenetic summons ("Watch!"), words about Jesus' destiny (Mk 14:21a, 62: death and exaltation to the right hand of God), and, in perhaps a later addition, also prophetic signs (the fig tree, the cleaning of the temple), conflict stories and parables (the tenants of the vineyard), and so on. Doubtless the kerygma of the death of Jesus for the many and of his vindication by God in his resurrection is woven into these narratives to form a whole fabric that cannot be unraveled. Hence, it seems to be much more probable that there was much cross-fertilization between the local churches in Jerusalem, Galilee and Syria. There may have been different emphases in them, but one is hard pressed to demonstrate that either the kerygma of the death and resurrection or the sayings of Jesus were unknown in any of them.[8]

(b) Pre-Markan Narratives

There seems, however, to be one tradition that had not been taken up in the passion story or in the kerygma of the church[9]—the tradition of the mighty deeds of Jesus, especially of his healings. An Israelite healed from a long-lasting disease did not simply go back to his work. He brought a thanksgiving offering or paid a priest to do so. He also testified to God's deed in the community of the believers, either immediately after his healing and/or in the synagogue on the sabbath. In a world without newspapers and radios, the story was gradually spread in the town and merchants soon carried it to other towns. Thus, Jesus' deeds became known. There is even a pattern that developed: it was usually reported how Jesus came in town, met the sick person, how long that illness had lasted or how serious it was, what Jesus then said or how he acted, how the suffering one was healed so that many people could see it, and how they all praised God. Similar stories are also to be found among Hellenistic Gentiles, although collections of them are rare and seem to postdate the gospels.[10] The main difference between the Jesus stories and similar stories is the

---

[8]At least, it would have been as Walter Schmithals (*Paulus und Jakobus*, Forschungen zur Religion und Literatur des Alten und Neuen Testaments 85 [1963] 25n5, 97-98) suggested long ago: a mother church in Galilee, from which the Q tradition stems, would have lived beside its daughter church in Jerusalem, in which the death and resurrection of Jesus became central. Cf. also my essay in *Horizons in Biblical Theology* 7 (1985).

[9]Acts 2:22; 10:38 are probably Lukan formulations.

[10]Paul J. Achtemeier, "The Origin and Function of the Pre-Marcan Miracle Catena," *Journal of Biblical Literature* 91 (1972): 200-202.

place of faith within the normal pattern. Hellenists would summon the hearer
to believe in the miracle-worker on the basis of the story. In the Jesus-stories,
however, faith (sometimes created by Jesus' way of addressing the sufferer)
usually precedes the healing.[11]

When Jesus spoke a word of interpretation in the context of such happen-
ings as Luke 11:20 ("When I cast out demons with the finger of God, the kingdom of God has come over you"), it prompted new hopes and was reported
together with the story. Even without such a word, the story was set into the
context of the ministry of Jesus to throw light on the whole of his activity. Thus,
stories of miraculous healings had been told and retold and had, more and more,
served to illustrate the specific authority of Jesus. They had even been collected. It is almost certain that the *Fourth Gospel* used a *signs source* which contained the miracle of changing water into wine (reported as the first sign of Jesus
in Jn 2:11), the healing of the son of the official, (reported as the second one
in Jn 4:54, cf. 46a, though, according to Jn 2:23; 3:2 Jesus had done many signs
before that), and other signs like that of the feeding the five thousand, also reported in the Synoptics. Such a source may have ended in a manner similar to
what we read in John 20:30-31: "Jesus did many other signs . . . , but these
are written that you may believe that Jesus is the Christ, the Son of God." A
similar source must have been known to Mark, since his own attitude toward
the miracles of Jesus is ambiguous, as I shall show presently. If the author of
the Fourth Gospel did not know the Synoptic gospels, it might be that a col-
lecton of signs and the passion story, perhaps even combined in one source,[12]
led him to write a gospel as it had led Mark to do before him. Be this as it may,
there is, again, no doubt that these miracle stories were intended to create faith.
Possibly, Jesus was presented in terms of a "man of God" like Elijah or Elisha,
in whom God's power became manifest. We do not know, however, whether
such a Christology ever existed in post-Easter times without the story of Jesus'
death and resurrection, let alone whether there was ever a group that concentrated exclusively on this aspect of Jesus' ministry.

Another important tradition is common to Q, to Mark and to John: Jesus
had disciples following him. In contrast to the common practice of the Jewish
rabbis, Jesus does not wait until young men come to him asking for permission
to follow him, but in a most unexpected way calls people to follow him.[13] Furthermore, the student of a rabbi hoped to become a rabbi himself, as famous
or even more famous than his teacher; yet no disciple of Jesus ever dreamed of

---

[11]Cf. Gerd Theissen, *Urchristliche Wundergeschichten*, Studien zum Neuen Testament 8 (Gütersloh: Gütersloher Verlag, 1974) 133-42.

[12]Cf. Gerhard Sellin, "Das Leben des Gottessohns," *Kairos* 25 (1983): 237-53.

[13]Q tells about men coming to Jesus (Mt 8:19-22), but emphasizes only Jesus' warning against following him and does not report whether or not they became his disciples.
The words to the disciples sent out by Jesus (Lk 10:2-12) prove, however, that Q presupposes a group of disciples surrounding Jesus.

becoming a Christ or a Son of Man himself. The rabbi and his followers formed a kind of school of exegesis of the Scripture in which the rabbi taught his disciples hermeneutical rules. Jesus did nothing of that kind, but let his disciples share with him his own experiences and his life with God. Therefore, the tradition of Jesus' call has become like a woodcut, which only preserves the few really essential traits (Mk 1:16-18, 19-20; 2:14; similarly Lk 19:5-6):[14] *Jesus* is "passing along" (he does not select auditors of his first sermon, Mk 1:14-15, but goes on to two fishermen); *Jesus* "sees" men at their everyday work (as God "sees" Israel or David, electing them to salvation or to a specific office); *Jesus* "calls" them (and only then do they realize that something is to happen to them); and it is *his* authority that creates their obedient response to leave whatever they are doing and to go with him ("*I* will make you become fishers of men"). Again, the call of Elisha by Elijah is the only Old Testament parallel, though it is a call to a specific office ordered by God himself (1 Kings 19:19-21).

Thus, a wide variety of traditions existed before our canonical gospels were written, some emphasizing the sayings of Jesus, some telling the story of his passion and resurrection, some reporting his stupendous deeds, some relating his call of disciples, and all of them, as far as we can see, proclaiming him as the final and definitive manifestation of God's grace-full coming to his people. There was no danger that the historical roots of the Christology would be forgotten so that faith would become mere ideology. Narratives deal, necessarily, with events that happened in a certain place at a certain time, so long as they are not transformed into mere mythological illustrations of an ideological truth. Neither was there the danger of a really Ebionite Christology, in which Jesus would simply have been a human being among others. Yet, the question remained as to whether the pattern of a wise teacher, of a suffering righteous one or of a miracle worker was the best to express that decisive presence of God in Jesus. The evangelists tried to answer this question in their gospels.

(c) Mark

In all four gospels words of the crucified Jesus have been handed down to us. These texts are a good starting point for an examination of each gospel's theology. Mark knows of one word only: "My God, my God, why hast thou forsaken me?" (Mk 15:34). The sun ceases to shine, darkness covers the earth, and Jesus dies with a loud cry. A Gentile with impure hands who had just executed an innocent man confesses: "Truly, this man was the Son of God." He sees nothing but darkness and suffering. He could not see that the curtain in the temple had torn in two revealing the most holy place where God himself lives. Mark paints the horror of this death, which is not merely a physical suffering but incomparably more a spiritual suffering: Jesus dies in total loneli-

---

[14]Jn 1:35-51 has transposed the stories into the time after Easter, when it is not the earthly Jesus, but his witness that is calling people to him, who in their turn, will call others, using Christological titles and Old Testament texts to qualify Jesus.

ness. Not one of his friends was there—some women "looking from afar," that's all. Nobody could carry on the cause of God. Thus, God himself must have collapsed. And yet, according to Mark, Jesus had said, "The Son of man has come . . . to serve and to give his life as a ransom for many" (Mk 10:45). On the evening before his death, Mark's Jesus had spoken of "my blood . . . poured out for many," and, on the cross, he still addresses God as "*my* God."

The cross overshadows the whole of Mark's gospel. The prologue (Mk 1:1-13) serves to qualify Jesus as the one who fulfills the prophecies of the Old Testament[15] and is designated by God's own voice as his son. After this, his Galilean ministry is divided in two parts by Peter's confession. Both parts consist of three sections. In the first half they begin, three times, with a short summary of Jesus' preaching and healing, followed either by his call of the first disciples, or by his selection of the twelve or his sending them out (Mk 1:14-15, 16-20; 3:7-12, 13-19; 6:6b, 7-13). All three sections end with the rejection of Jesus, first by the Pharisees and Herodians (Mk 3:6), then by his fellow-citizens (Mk6:1-6a), finally by his own disciples, to whom he quotes the prophetic condemnation used in chapter 4 (verse 12) against those outside who cannot understand him: "Having eyes you do not see, and having ears you do not hear" (Mk 8:14-21). Then follows a short story of the healing of a blind man, which shows that it is God alone who can open blind eyes (Mk 8:22-26), leading to the confession of Peter: "You are the Christ" (Mk 8:27-29). This confession, however, is not so central in Mark as in Matthew; Peter has not even reached the level of the demons who had long before recognized the "Son of God," and Jesus neither rejects nor accepts Peter's confession, but reformulates it at once by speaking of the Son of man who is to suffer. Three predictions of his rejection, suffering, death and resurrection frame the second half of Jesus' ministry (Mk 8:31; 9:30-32; 10:32-34). Each prediction is followed by a total misunderstanding on the part of the disciples. First, Peter urges Jesus not to go to Jerusalem and is rebuked: "Get behind me, Satan. For you are not on the side of God, but of men" (Mk 8:32-33). Second, the disciples discuss—immediately after the prediction of the crucifixion!—who among them will be the greatest (Mk 9:33-34). Third, James and John ask for the best seats in heaven (Mk 10:35-37). All three times, Jesus answers with a new summons to follow him in genuine discipleship. At the end of the third section follows again a short story of the healing of a blind man, symbolizing the fact that God alone can open blind eyes (Mk 10:46-52). The last words before the passion story begins are "And he [the healed blind man] followed him on the road." That this has a symbolic connotation is evident, because it echoes what was said of the disciples just 20 verses earlier, introducing the last prediction of the crucifixion: "They were on the road, going up to Jerusalem, and Jesus was walking ahead of them . . . and those who followed were afraid." Then follows the passion story (Mk 11-16).

---

[15]The texts cited in Mk 1:2-3 are the only explicit Scripture quotations referred to by the evangelist himself.

It is remarkable that apart from this symbolic story, parallel to that at the end of the first half of the gospel (Mk 8:22-26), Mark includes no miracle story in the second half of Jesus' ministry. The healing of the epileptic boy in 9:14-29 is actually a treatise about the right kind of faith, for which the healing provides the occasion. It contains the discussion with the father who prays, "I believe, help my unbelief," and with the disciples who ask, "Why could we not cast it out?" Thus, miracles are important to Mark as signs pointing to the significance of Jesus; but only the one who looks at the crucified Jesus, where no miracle happens and all remains dark, and only the one who is ready to follow him on this road is able to understand these signs. They are but a kind of preliminary revelation, leading to the first open and clear (Mk 8:32![16]) revelation in the prediction of the suffering of the Son of man.

In many ways this is a very modern approach. No longer do we think, like our fathers in the last century, that nothing could happen that could not be explained rationally. There was an Indian in Zurich years ago who got a dagger driven through the center of his heart and lived on as if nothing had happened. Colleagues of the medical faculty came to the man, examined him and x-rayed him. There was no trick; the miracle had happened, but—and this is the essential point nobody "believes" in this Indian because of this. According to Mark the one miracle is that God does not remain silent forever but is revealing himself to us, saying his word through the ministry of Jesus up to his death, and reaching our hearts so that a Gentile who sees nothing but the death of a dreadfully exhausted young man may see the Son of God. This is *the* miracle. Nonetheless, healing and so on are not unimportant. They are like signs on a highway that warn us: "Look out for a coming curve!" We should see the danger without a special sign, but sometimes we are inattentive. In the same way, God sometimes has to use unusual ("miraculous") means to approach us because we are too foolish to listen to him, to trust in him and his word without them. This is what Luke understands when he tells us that Jesus said the usual closing sentence of a healing story "Your faith has made you well" only to the one of the ten lepers who came back to praise God (Lk 17:19) and to the prostitute who experienced no physical healing at all (Lk 7:50). In both cases the Greek word has regained its full sense: "Your faith has saved you."

(d) Matthew

In Matthew we find the same saying of Jesus on the cross. But Matthew has emended Mark in Matthew 27:34, saying that the wine given to Jesus was "mingled with gall" because this was predicted in Psalm 69:22. He has also introduced the wording of Psalm 22:9 in Matthew 27:43 to show that this shocking way of dying is God's will, declared already centuries before. Matthew then describes an earthquake that took place when Jesus died. It split the

---

[16]In contrast to (Mk 2:2 and) 4:33, where the same Greek phrase appears. See now Dan O. Via, Jr., *The Ethics of Mark's Gospel—in the Middle of Time* (Philadelphia: Fortress Press, 1985) esp. 177, 190-93.

rocks and opened the tombs so that the bodies came out and went into the holy city. When the Roman officer sees this, he speaks in confession. Thus, Matthew is not satisfied with the puzzling expression of faith found in Mark. He is interested in a visible vindication of Jesus by God, perhaps because he knows better than Mark that the death on the cross is, according to the Mosaic law, cursed by God. Galatians 3:13 and the Dead Sea Scrolls (11 Q Temple 64:12) prove that this curse of Deuteronomy 21:23 is still very much on the minds of Jews contemporary to Jesus.

Throughout his gospel Matthew shows his concern with regard to the question of the law. The structure of his gospel (except for chapters 5-9) follows that of Mark, with the insertion of new material in various places. In chapters 5-7 he collects sayings of Jesus, which were (according to Luke) spoken at various occasions, into one long sermon (on the mount). In chapters 8-9 he does much the same with various deeds of Jesus, especially healings. At the end of chapter 9 he adds two short reports of two blind men and a deaf[17] man healed by Jesus, which are actually duplicates of the healings told later in Matthew 20:30-34 and 12:22-24. Careful examination reveals the reason for this. In Matthew 11:4-5 Jesus tells the two disciples of John the Baptist who ask him whether he is the one to come or not: "Go and tell John what you hear and see: The blind receive their sight and the lame walk, lepers are cleansed and the deaf hear, and the dead are raised up, and the poor have good news preached to them." The latter has been described in the Sermon on the Mount (Mt 5-7), which begins: "Blessed are the poor"; the former in Matthew 8-9, including the last two healings, which Matthew did not find elsewhere and therefore had to duplicate from later stories (which he needed again in their later context). Before coming to the prophecy of Isaiah in chapter 11, he inserts chapter 10 in order to show that the church shares the authority of Jesus to preach and to heal[18] as the disciples demonstrate in their mission. Thus, the picture of Jesus and his church, fulfilling the law and the prophets, is central to Matthew. The same becomes obvious in the Matthean structure of the Sermon on the Mount. After the introduction by the beatitudes and summons to the hearers Matthew starts with the statement of Jesus: "I have not come to abolish the law and the prophets but to fulfill them." He closes, before adding some warnings against false prophets and the parable of the house built on the rock, with the golden rule and the remark: "This is the law and the prophets." He also adds to the Markan text in Matthew 22:39-40 the remark that the commandment to love one's neighbor is equal to the first, to love God, and that "all the law and the prophets hinge upon these two rules." In Matthew 19:19 he supplements the commandments of the decalogue quoted in the discussion with the rich ruler

---

[17]The Greek word in Mt 9:32-33 and 11:4 describes a "deaf and dumb" man.

[18]Mt 10:1: "to heal every disease and every infirmity" is literally identical with what was said of Jesus four verses earlier, and 10:7-8 combines preaching and healing in the activity of the church, as it is typical of the ministry of Jesus.

with the command to love one's neighbor and in Matthew 9:13 and in 12:7 he inserts God's criterion ("I desire mercy and not sacrifice") into the Markan text.

This editing represents the Matthean solution of the problem of the law. As the constitution of a state is superior to specific local legislation and when a conflict arises, settles the case, so the commandment to love one's neighbor is superior to the single rules of the law. Hence, the Matthean church is, probably, still keeping the Sabbath and does not violate this commandment even in cases of danger to life (Mt 24:20 compared with Mk 13:18), but it has given up food regulations because they prevent the nations from entering the covenant of God.

Matthean constructions are again visible in chapters 21-24. The conflict stories in Jerusalem are connected in the way of a chain. A typical phrase of the first story is repeated in the second, one of the second in the third, and one of the third in the fourth.[19] They describe the trial of Israel. The interrogation of the defendant (Mt 21:24-27: Who was John the Baptist?) is followed by his conviction (Mt 21:31-32: as of the son who said yes but did not do it), the sentence determining the punishment (Mt 21:40-43: the vineyard will be given to others) and its execution (Mt 22:7: the king destroyed their city). The same chain of events is repeated in Matthew 22:15-24:51.[20] Both times, however, the essential point made by Matthew is the warning of the church—exactly the same fate will befall it if it is not obedient to the will of its lord. This is shown by the man without a wedding garment at the end of the first sequence and by the warnings of the eschatological sermon at the end of the second sequence. In both pericopes the same threat is repeated: "There men will weep and gnash their teeth" (Mt 22:13, 24:51, both times closing the whole sequence).

Even more important is the identification of Jesus with Wisdom, shown by the redactional changes in Matthew 11:2, 19 ("Wisdom is justified by her deeds," meaning "the deeds of the Christ"!), by the quotation of the call of Wisdom: "Come to me all who labor and are heavy laden" (11:28-30; cf. Ben Sirach 51:23-27), and by the fact that the word of Wisdom (Lk 11:49) becomes in Matthew that of Jesus (Mt 23:34). Thus Jesus' "I say to you" can stand over against the word of God, as "it was said to the men of old," because the Word of God (often identified with his Wisdom) has become incarnated in Jesus (Mt 5:21-48). Matthew could write, as the Fourth Gospel does in John 1:14, "The Word has become flesh," but it would locate that incarnation in the authoritative teaching of Jesus in which he is with his disciples "always to the close of the age" wherever they "teach what he has commanded" (Mt 28:20). The core of this teaching is, as I have shown, love toward one's neighbor. Matthew sees it manifested in an outstanding, unique way in the death of Jesus "as a ransom for many" (Mt 20:28), in "the blood poured out for many for the forgiveness

---

[19]"You did not believe him" (John the Baptist) Mt 21:26,32; "the kingdom of God" (very unusual in Matthew!) Mt 21:31,43; "he sent his servants . . . again he sent other servants," Mt 21:34-36, 22:3, 4.

[20]Mt 22:15-46; 23:1-32,33-6; 23:27–24:2.

of sins" (as Matthew adds in Mt 26:28), and in the new encounter of the risen Lord with his disciples and their new commitment after their failure (Mt 28:18-20).

(e) Luke

The three Lukan sayings show the crucified Lord turning toward his fellowmen in their guilt and need: "Father, forgive them, for they know not what they do," "Today you will be with me in paradise" (Lk 23:34, 43), and to his father in heaven: "Father, into thy hands I commit my spirit" (Lk 23:46). Thus, he is the love and forgiveness of God himself that visits his people. Therefore, Luke's gospel starts with the experience of an elderly childless couple and God's gift to them, which forshadows the experience of Mary and God's gift to her and to all humankind (Lk 1:5-2:40). In his inaugural sermon in Nazareth (Lk 4:18) Jesus reveals himself as the preacher of good news to the poor and as liberator of the captives foretold by Isaiah. He brings the sinner back into God's love. There is Peter who cries out, "Depart from me, for I am a sinful man" (Lk 5:8), and the prostitute who anoints him and whose many sins have been forgiven (Lk 7:47-48). The parables of the lost sheep, the lost coin, and the prodigal son (Lk 15), of the vindicated widow, the Pharisee, and the tax collector (Lk 18:1-14) are reported only by Luke. He alone tells of women following Jesus in Galilee (Lk 8:1-3), and together with Zecharias we find Mary (Lk 1:11-2, 27-29, 46, 67), with Simeon, Anna (Lk 2:25, 36). With the father of a dead daughter we find the mother of a dead son (Lk 8:41, 7:12) and with the scribe we find the two sisters (Lk 10:25-37, 38-42). With the insistent man we find the insistent widow (Lk 11:5-7; 18:1-8), and with the man healed on the sabbath we find the woman healed on the sabbath (Lk 14:1-7, 13:10-17). With the son of Abraham we find the daughter of Abraham (Lk 19:9, 13:16), while with the parable of the shepherd we find the parable of the woman (Lk 15:3-7, 8-10). With the man who sows the mustard seed we find the woman who hides the leaven (Lk 13:19-21 Q).

Typical of the structure of Luke's gospel is the long journey to Jerusalem.[21] First, Luke omits the saying of Jesus that he came to give his life as a ransom for many (Mk 10:45) and replaces it with "I am among you as one who serves" (Lk 22:27), which emphasizes that his whole life, not merely his death, is important to faith.[22] Second, Stephen echoes in his martyrdom the two words of the crucified Jesus: "Lord, do not hold this sin against them" and "Lord Jesus, receive my spirit" (Acts 7:60, 59). This opens our eyes to the similarity of

---

[21]It begins in Lk 9:51: "He set his face to go to Jerusalem." This is emphasized in Lk 13:22, 33 ("a prophet is to die in Jerusalem") and again in Lk 17:11 ("on the way to Jerusalem") until Jesus is "near to Jerusalem" (Lk 19:11) and had to warn against illusionary expectations of a coming kingdom.

[22]Cf. also Lk 19:10 ("The Son of Man came to seek and to save the lost") which at the same place as Mk 10:45 points again to his whole ministry, not merely to his death.

the journey of Paul and his captivity to that of Jesus.[23] For Luke, faith is *a way to go*, and the experiences of the believer on this journey will shadow those of Jesus. This does not mean that the believer is journeying on an equal level with Jesus. Whereas Jesus commits his spirit to the Father, Stephen commits his spirit to his Lord Jesus because it is only Jesus' death that makes Stephen's way possible. Luke also knows of "the blood poured out for you"[24] though he just repeats the phrase without connecting it with its context.[25] Like Matthew, Luke tells the story of the virgin birth of Jesus so that he is qualified as the unique Son of God from the very beginning. But while Matthew sees the salvation history of God reaching its goal in this birth through three times fourteen generations, Luke sees it as the fulfllment of experiences of faithful people in the time of the Old Testament and up to his time.[26]

(f) John

In the Fourth Gospel Jesus dies as the victor. Even on the cross he is still the ruling Lord, giving to his mother a son and to his beloved disciple a mother (Jn 19:26-27). The second word "I thirst" is merely said "to fulfill the scripture" (Jn 19:28), and his last word is "It is accomplished" (Jn 19:30). In this gospel, "the child of sorrow of New Testament scholarship,"[27] almost everything is disputable. Does the author fight Gnosticism in Gnostic terminology (Bultmann) or is he himself a Gnostic with a naively docetic Christology (Käsemann, Schottroff)? Is it a Christology of the messenger of God, a prophet, an angel (Ian Bühner), or a conglomerate of various layers contradicting one another (G. Richter, M. E. Boismard)?[28] Personally, I think that Louis Mar-

---

[23]Time and again, Paul's journey to Jerusalem is underlined (Acts 19:21; 20:22; 21:4, 11-15), and the sequence of prediction of his suffering, farewell discourse, and trial before the high priest, the Roman governor, and the Herodian king (Acts 9:16; 20:18-25, 22:30; 23:23; 25:23) parallels that of the passion of Jesus in Luke's gospel.

[24]The RSV of 1952 omits Lk 22:19b-20, probably wrongly; that of 1971 includes them, but omits, strangely enough, the phrase "poured out for you," which seems to be in all the manuscripts that include verses 19b-20.

[25]Nominative case instead of dative! Similarly, the liturgical phrase "of his blood" is, in Acts 20:28, mechanically added to the context so that it speaks literally of the blood of God instead of that of Jesus.

[26]Lk 3:23-38 also reports a genealogical tree of Jesus. It is still visible that, originally, 11 times 7 generations leads to him, the beginning of the twelfth "week" of generations, of the messianic "week," but Luke either did not know that or was not interested in it, since he does not point to it at all. This means that salvation history is taught in the prologue of Matthew, but not in Luke, if we define "salvation history" as a history that is planned in detail, step by step, from the very beginning to the final goal, by God himself.

[27]J. Becker, *Oekumenischer Taschenbuchkommentar*, 4/1, 27.

[28]See the evidence in Eduard Schweizer, "Jesus Christus," in *Theologische Realenzyklopädie* (Berlin: Walter de Gruyter, 1976–) §7.1.

tyn has opened a viable road when he tried to detect the historic situation of the Johannine community behind many details of this gospel.[29] They are facing persecution, ostracism, and martyrdom (Jn 9:22,34; 16:1-2). Klaus Wengst suggested that after A.D. 70 this was only possible beyond the Jordan, east of Northern Galilee.[30] This would explain the emphasis on the divine status of Jesus since his earthly ministry was common knowledge to all parties in the conflict. At any rate, they knew existentially what martyrdom meant and would certainly not identify the crucified Jesus with "a God striding across the earth."[31]

Despite many various patterns in the background—the Logos, the miracle worker, the Son of Man, the Passover lamb, the messenger, the indwelling wisdom—the essential fact is that the author wrote a gospel, neither a treatise nor a myth. God's presence among men is not an idea, for God "became flesh"[32] in a man's life with all its ups and downs, which John sees as the life of "the lamb that takes away the sin of the world" (Jn 1:29 at the beginning of the gospel) and of the Passover lamb, whose bones are not broken (Jn 19:36 at its end). Though incarnation leads to a vision of glory (Jn 1:14), it is to be seen in his earthly life, not in the resurrection. Though his opponents are not specified (like Pharisees against tax collectors in the Synoptics) they are a historical nation, the "Jews," and only in the farewell discourse "the world" (in exactly the same position). Though his crucifixion is understood as exaltation, it is because, on the cross, his will has become definitively one with that of the Father. All this is very different from Gnosticism, which is not interested at all in the earthly Jesus, not even in his miracles or speeches, but only in the revelation of the Risen One, whereas in the Fourth Gospel it is the paraclete, not the risen Lord, who comes to his disciples and reminds them of the words of the earthly Jesus.[33] And what is the content of these words? Not the kingdom of God, but throughout the "I" of Jesus: "I am the bread of life, the good shepherd, the true vine, the way, the truth, the life." Grammatically, "I" is in the predicative position. This means that it gives answer to the question of where

---

[29]J. Louis Martyn, *History and Theology in the Fourth Gospel* (Nashville: Abingdon, 1979).

[30]Klaus Wengst, *Bedrängte Gemeinde und verherrlichter Christus*, Biblisch-theologische Studien 5 (1981).

[31]Ernst Käsemann, *Jesu letzter Wille nach Johannes* 17 (Tübingen: J. C. B. Mohr, 1966); repeated by S. Schulz, *Das Evangelium nach Johannes*, Das Neue Testament Deutsch 4 (1972) 224.

[32]In the view of John Painter ("Christology and the History of the Johannine Community in the Prologue of the Fourth Gospel," *New Testament Studies* 30 [1984]: 468, 470) the incarnation is even emphasized by the evangelist, who fought against a docetic Christology. Joseph Blank ("Die Irrlehrer des ersten Johannesbriefs," *Kairos* 26 [1984]: 175) speaks plausibly of "Einwohnungschristologie" (a Christology of inhabitation [of God in Jesus]).

[33]Jn 14:26; 6:63; 15:3, 7; 8:31, 51; 12:48; 14:23.

man will find real bread, real guidance, real life. Mankind is searching for all this, and the Johannine Jesus answers: "*I* am the true vine, the good shepherd, the living bread." According to Paul, justification means that *Jesus* is *the* righteousness that man is striving after, or in the case of the Corinthians, *the* wisdom. John expands this answer: whatever man is searching for, *Jesus is the* bread, *the* vine, *the* shepherd, *the* life. Whatever our view is, whether Jewish or Gnostic opponents suggested these terms, whether Jesus' humanity was the basis granted by both parties or was not taken seriously enough, whether the Johannine Christ was close to or remote from the real Jesus of Nazareth, what the Fourth Gospel wants to convey to its readers is the earthly existence of Jesus, in whose acts and words God himself has encountered mankind in definitive salvation, and in whom the truth has become historical reality.

Chapter 4

JESUS OF NAZARETH AS GOD'S CHRIST

(a) The Hermeneutical Circle from the Kerygma to Jesus and Back

In the first chapter I detected a growing consensus that both the picture of the earthly Jesus and the post-Easter kerygma have to be taken seriously. In the second chapter I demonstrated that all the early creedal formulae and hymns in the New Testament emphasize the events marginal to the earthly life of Jesus which qualify it as God's unique presence. In the third chapter I showed that Jesus' sayings were, as early as in Q, set into the context of his life, and his deeds were understood as signs of his unique position. This means that the question put by the Easter event is the same question put by every saying or deed of Jesus: is it, as the kerygma says and as the way of collecting his sayings and his deeds implicitly shows, God's own act that qualifies the ministry of Jesus up to his death as the decisive saving action of God? When Jesus invites a tax collector to his table, is this merely a neglecting of social barriers or is it an event demonstrating the forgiveness of sins that brings the tax collector back into the covenant of God? The gospels answer in the latter sense because they share the conviction of the post-Easter church that Jesus' resurrection has qualified him, even in his death, as the savior of the world. Is this consistent with what we know of the earthly Jesus? Is the conviction of the post-Easter church a misunderstanding, at best an independent interpretation appended to the life of this first-century Jew? Is the conviction of the post-Easter church a possible, even a reasonable, assumption? Or is it *the* truth?

(b) The Kerygma in Jesus' Own Teaching

It is shocking to realize that, according to the Synoptic gospels, Jesus never called himself the messiah. Mark 12:35 deals with the assumption of the scribes that the messiah be David's son, without direct connection with Jesus. Mark 9:41 ("because you bear the name of Christ") is a later version of Matthew 10:42 ("because he is a disciple"). Matthew 23:10 ("one is your master, the Christ") is a Hellenistic variant of verse 8 ("one is your teacher [rabbi]"). Mark 13:21 (Mt 24:5) and Luke 24:46 belong to the post-Easter period. The confession of

Peter, "You are the Christ," and the question of the high priest, "Are you the Christ?" (Mk 8:29; 14:61) may well be historical,[1] but in both cases one other than Jesus uses the term, and though Jesus did not reject it, it is not clear that he accepted it unrestrictedly. Thus, Jesus very probably never proclaimed himself as the messiah; if he was addressed as such, he was rather reluctant to accept the title.

The same is true for the term "Son of God." The contrast of "the Father" to "the Son" is to be found in Mark 13:32 ("Of that day [the parousia] . . . no one knows, not even the angels in heaven, nor the Son, but only the Father") and in Matthew 11:27 ("No one knows the Son except the Father").[2] This certainly implies the divine sonship of Jesus; however, the emphasis is different. When we speak of the Son of God we distinguish him from a son of human parents and underline his superiority. When Jesus speaks of "the Son," who is not "the Father," he expresses (in his time!) his subordination, his unpretentiousness.

Finally, the title "Servant of God," so full of meaning since the time of Deutero-Isaiah (53:5: "wounded for our trespasses . . . bruised for our iniquities"!) appears only in Acts 3-4. Though Isaiah 53 played a considerable role in the early Christian tradition, even there it is a somewhat ambiguous role. In Acts 3, for example, it refers to the suffering servant, while in Acts 4 it refers to the royal representative of God.

There is but one title that Jesus may have used when speaking of himself, just because in his time it was not a title: Son of Man. The problems surrounding the meaning of this title are far from being solved and perhaps never will be. In the Old Testament "son of man" is the usual term for an individual man, since "Adam" ("man") means primarily "humankind" (Ps 8:5, et al.). In Ezekiel God addresses the prophet about 87 times as "son of man." Finally, Daniel introduces in his vision first four empires symbolized by four different beasts, then Israel as the people of God in the image of a "son of man" flying on the clouds to God, either horizontally or from below, certainly not from heaven to earth (Dan 7:13). It is impossible to determine whether such a figure was already known to the author or whether he chose it simply as a symbol in contrast to the beasts. In Judaism, 4 (2) Ezra 13:3 (not earlier than the end of the first century A.D.) tells of a savior who is "something like a son of man" coming up out of the sea.[3] However, the New Testament speaks, with the ex-

---

[1] I think they are. The rebuke of Peter as Satan is scarcely invented. It could not, originally, have immediately corresponded with his confession of Jesus as Christ, for who in the early church would have handed down such a tradition? Thus, some prediction of suffering must have been uttered by Jesus, and some kind of messianic hope among his disciples may have caused it. The word in the trial is more questionable, since it is difficult to know what witness would have reported it; still, some priests became Christians after Easter and may have told the story of Jesus' trial.

[2] The authority of both passages is disputed, probably wrongly.

[3] The interpretation of the vision in 4 Ezra 13:32 identifies this "man" with the "servant (or Son?) of God."

ception of Revelation 1:13; 14:14, of *the* Son of Man (with both articles in Greek[4]). This is only comparable to the use in Ethiopic (1) Enoch 37-71, an Ethiopic translation of a Greek translation of a Semitic original the authenticity of which is debatable.[5] Moreover, the date of these chapters is unknown. They could have been written in the Christian era. An origin of the figure of the son of man in any of the Palestinian religions outside of Judaism is very improbable.[6] Thus, it is very difficult to determine whether a more or less fixed figure of a mythic Son of Man was known to Judaism at the time of Jesus.

In the New Testament, Q, Mark and the special material of both Matthew and Luke, portray the Son of Man as the coming judge. In Q and Mark, the Son of Man is also the earthly Jesus in his humiliation (Q) or his authority (Mark). Finally in Mark, and in a secondary way also in passages unique to Matthew and Luke, the Son of Man is the suffering Jesus. With the exception of Acts 7:56 the term appears only on the lips of Jesus.[7] Five main solutions having many variations have been proposed as solutions to this problem.

1. First, it has been suggested that the title was introduced by the post-Easter church. This suggestion is based on the fact that Jesus avoided titles when speaking of himself, let alone titles connected with apocalyptic descriptions of the future. Furthermore, the final coming of the Son of Man is not combined with the predictions of Jesus' death and resurrection. How then could Jesus speak of his coming from heaven while still on earth? Against this suggestion is the fact that the title "Christ" is to be found more than 500 times in the New Testament but practically never on the lips of Jesus. Might prophets, speaking in the name of the risen Lord, have introduced the title? Revelation 2-3 contain words of the risen Lord formulated in the first person, introduced, however, by the prophetic formula "Thus speaks [with a circumscription of the risen Christ]" and closed by the indication that it is the Spirit who speaks through the prophet. It is, however, questionable whether such words of a prophet were

---

[4]This would correspond to the *status emphaticus* in Aramaic.

[5]For instance, there appears "a man" (using once the term for man in general, once the other one for a male person), a figure of some importance, in the vision of 1 Enoch 89 (1 and 9), but the term "man" is lacking in the Aramaic fragment of one of these verses, showing that the Greek or the Ethiopic translator has added it to the original text, which does not know the term.

[6]Carsten Colpe, "υἱὸς τοῦ ἀνθρώπου," *Theological Dictionary of the New Testament*, 10 vols., ed. Gerhard Friedrich, trans. Geoffrey Bromiley (Grand Rapids: Eerdmans, 1964-1976) 8: 415-20. Wolfgang Bittner ("Gott-Menschensohn-Davidssohn," *Freiburger Zeitschrift für Philosophie und Theologie* 32 [1985]: 343-72) suggests that the clouds of Dan 7:13 point to a theophany, 7:14 to the messiah (or, I should add, to the eschatological Israel; cf. Jub 1:24-25) so that the Son of Man would be a kind of angel in whom God himself (cf. Ezek 1:26) turns toward his people.

[7]In Jn 12:34, the people just repeat the title used by Jesus in verse 23. The evidence in John shows all three ways of using the title if we suppose that Jn 5:27 originally spoke of the last judgment.

ever accepted as equal to words of the earthly Jesus,[8] and one must also ask why this title would have been used exclusively by prophets.

2. A second suggestion argues that Jesus spoke of the coming Son of man without identifying himself with that figure. This hypothesis is based on Luke 12:8: "Everyone who acknowledges me before men, the Son of Man also will acknowledge before the angels of God."[9] In considering this proposal one must reckon with the difficulty of imagining that the words and deeds of Jesus[10] would proffer the expectation of one superior to himself other than God. Furthermore, one must ask why the Easter experiences would have led the disciples to identify that greater one with Jesus. Why not simply confirm the truth of the prophecy of Jesus? The shift from the first to the third person in Luke 12:8 is quite natural. Experiences of transcendence are easily put in the third person as Paul shows in 1 Corinthians 12:2: "*I* know a *man* [in Semitic idiom: a son of man]," meaning himself.[11]

3. Third, British scholars, along with Norman Perrin and others in North America,[12] consider "Son of Man" a corporate title for both Jesus and the New Israel created by Jesus. Support for this view is found in Daniel's identification of the Son of man with Israel. This would also explain the concept in John 1:51 of the Son of man as the new Jacob-Israel. There is also the identification of Jesus as the vine (the symbol of Israel) embodying his disciples as branches and, perhaps most significantly, the Pauline idea of the body of Christ. This view, however, fails to account for the clearly individual status of the Son of Man in many sayings of Jesus.[13] The Son of Man rejected by this generation is seen as parallel with John the Baptist in Luke 7:34 Q (where both are still seen on the same level!) or with Jonah in Luke 11:30 Q, and especially the already-quoted word about the Son of Man acknowledging those who have sided with him (Lk 12:8 Q, also Mk 8:38 and other texts).

4. Personally, I am in agreement with those who think that Jesus spoke of himself as the Son of Man. The reason for this is the fact that the idea of an

---

[8]M. E. Boring, "Christian Prophecy and the Sayings of Jesus: The State of the Question," *New Testament Studies* 29 (1983): 104-12, and the articles cited there in n. 4; also J. D. G. Dunn, *Jesus and the Spirit* (London: SCM Press, 1975), 173-74, cf. 178-80.

[9]See references for both hypotheses in Günter Klein, "Eschatologie" *Theologische Realenzyklopädie* 10:272-73.

[10]Cf. §c in this chapter.

[11]Compare Niklaus von Flue (1417-1487) as cited by P. A. Wagner in *Der Geschichtsfreund* 83 (1928): 110, 112: "A man broke his sleep by God's will and because of his suffering" (my translation), though it is not quite clear whether this is a report by the saint himself.

[12]C. F. D. Moule, *The Origin of Christology* (Cambridge: Cambridge University Press, 1977) 11-21, 129-30, 152-58; Norman Perrin, *Jesus and the Language of the Kingdom* (Philadelphia: Fortress Press, 1976) 59.

[13]Also in 4 Ezra; see Colpe, "υἱὸς τοῦ ἀνθρώπου," 427-29.

earthly Son of Man, rejected and suffering, is not derivable from any Jewish or Christian group or writing. The sequence of suffering and death, vindication by God, exaltation to heaven, and activity as judge or as chief witness in the last judgment is part of the pattern of the destiny of the suffering righteous as early as in Wisdom 2:12-20; 4:10-17; and 5:1-5. Jesus could have taken up these expectations, using the term "Son of Man," precisely because it was not a fixed title,[14] and used it as a challenge to the hearer who was forced to ask whether this was a simple, though unusual, circumlocution for "I" or a symbol meaning much more. The argument against this solution is based on the lack of both a pre-Christian combination of Son of Man or even Servant of God with the suffering righteous (though Wisd 2-5 are influenced by Isa 53) and the absence of a clear connection of the parousia of the Son of Man with either his death and resurrection or the kingdom of God in the New Testament (though Lk 22:69 and Mk 14:62 on the one hand and Mk 8:38-9:1 on the other show, at least, a possibility of both connections).

5. In a recent publication[15] Werner Georg Kümmel has proposed a variation of and challenged my view. He is convinced that there was, in the time of Jesus, an apocalyptic concept of a Son of Man, based mainly on Daniel 7. Thus, the phrase was a kind of title for a saving figure to be expected at the end of the present age. Jesus took it up, exactly as he took up the term "kingdom of God," but in the same way as he changed its meaning totally by speaking of the presence of this kingdom, he also changed the meaning of the term "son of man." In both cases Jesus did not deny the future role of the kingdom and of the Son of Man. In fact, the future fulfillment remained most important. However, in both cases, he proclaimed that the future kingdom and the future coming of the Son of Man were already present in his words and deeds, though it was an open question as to whether or not people could see that presence.

I am not convinced of this solution, because unlike the idea of the kingdom of God, the expectation of the Son of Man, if it existed at all in the Judaism of the time of Jesus, was probably restricted to a small group of apocalypticists. Furthermore, the identification of Jesus with the personal figure of the Son of Man was of a different type compared with the identification of God's ruling in Jesus' preaching and healing with his eschatological ruling in the coming kingdom. Still I would never deny that this is a possible and even tempting solution and that Kümmel's essay is an excellent contribution to the discussion.

---

[14]Cf. Barnabas Lindars, *Jesus Son of Man* (London: SPCK, 1983) 44-47. A mistranslation of *bar-nasha* by "Son of Man" instead of "different from man" (G. Gerleman, "Der Menschensohn," *Studia Biblica* 1 [1983]: 13) is very improbable (cf. the Hebrew *ben-adam* = *adam*, Ps 8:5, et al.).

[15]Werner Georg Kümmel, *Jesus der Menschensohn?*, Sitzungsberichte der wissenschaftlichen Gesellschaft an der Johann Wolfgang Goethe Universität Frankfurt am Main 20/3 (Stuttgart: Franz Steiner Verlag, 1984).

The only thing we can say with some certainty is that Jesus either did not use the title Son of Man (1)[16]—at least not when speaking of himself (2)—or if he used it, changed its meaning totally (5), or that it was, in his time, not a title, but rather a challenging riddle that Jesus either connected with the corporate idea in Daniel 7—as answer 3 suggests—or used because it was ambiguous and could be understood in a simple way or as a pointer to various ideas (4).

(c) The Implicit Christology

Jesus probably never claimed the title "Christ." And yet he did what nobody ever expected the messiah to do. He healed all kinds of diseases; he called disciples to follow him (see chapter 3 [b:1-3]). He brought forgiveness of sins to men, with or without saying so, and transferred them back into the people of God (see chapter 4 [a]). He interpreted his activity as the presence of the kingdom of God, as something beyond the prophets and kings of the Bible (Lk 10:24; 11:32; see chapter 3 [b:2]). He spoke in parables with the idea that in them the kingdom itself was approaching his hearers (see chapter 3 [a:5]). He dared to declare that the worst sinners in the Scripture, Sodom and Gomorrah, would be better off in the last judgement than the town that rejected his call to repentance (Mt 11:20-24; see chapter 3 [a:4]). Finally, he did not use the formula of the prophetic messenger—"Thus says the Lord"—nor that of the teacher of the law—"It is written"—but he opened his sayings with "I say to you" and put his "I" even against the "I" of God himself, as it is found in the Scripture in God's own words (Mt 5:21-48).

Who is this man whose authority commands illness and obsession? Who is this man who claims that following him is the one decisive act in view of the coming kingdom, more important than caring for one's family and providing food for them? Who is this man who acts as if he were the almighty God himself, who alone has the authority to forgive sins? Who is this man who thinks that God's kingdom has been actualized in his words and deeds? Who is this man who sees in himself the manifestation of God's kingdom? Who is this man who thinks that failing to respond to him is worse than any other sin? Who is this man who puts himself on a plane equal to or even superior to the God of the Bible?

Second, Jesus never used the title "Son of God" when speaking of himself. And yet he calls God "Abba" (Mk 14:36; cf. Rom 8:15; Gal 4:6). The frequent

---

[16]This position is also that of a book published in the meantime: Walter Simonis, *Jesus von Nazareth. Seine Botschaft vom Reich Gottes und der Glaube der Urgemeinde* (Düsseldorf: Patmos-Verlag) ch. 5. According to Simonis the concept of the Son of man was developed gradually after Easter, not in the very first year. Since Peter had seen the risen Jesus—as the only one, by the way!—the disciples believed that he was still living and expected him to come and to bring the messianic kingdom in Israel, not later than at the next Passover. When he did not come within that first year, the church began to emphasize his exaltation to heaven. In a much later stage the title was also carried back to the earthly life of Jesus.

50 Jesus Christ

address "Father" probably goes back to the same Aramaic term.[17] It seems that Palestinian Jews did not address God as "Father" in their prayers before the time of Jesus, and after him they usually combined it with "our King." Within a prayer, as for instance in Isaiah 63:16 ("Thou art our Father, though Abraham does not know us . . . "), the term serves as a simile: He is the one who knows us, as a father knows his children. However, Hellenistic Jews occasionally address God as Father in prayers prior to Jesus,[18] and it is questionable whether the separation of Palestinian and Hellenistic Judaism can be maintained. Be that as it may, there is no doubt that "Abba" is used exclusively by Jesus and later on by his disciples. It is a term of intimacy used by children but also by adults, perhaps comparable to our "Daddy."

Other evidence for a unique relation of Jesus to his heavenly Father, though unfortunately scarce, must be considered. Jesus speaks either of "my Father" or of "your Father." The latter, however, appears only once in Mark (11:25) and twice in Q (Lk 6:36; 12:30). The former appears only once in Q (Lk 10:22) and implicity in Mark 8:38, which speaks of the glory of "his" (the Son of Man's) Father. Both phrases occur frequently in the material peculiar to Matthew and John and occasionally also Luke. While we cannot be completely sure, it appears that Jesus never shared the expression "our Father" with his disciples or other people; the Lord's Prayer in its Matthean form is explicitly given to the disciples: "*you* shall pray'Our Father' " and Luke knows only the address "Father." Again, who is this man who is convinced of a unique relation to God, his Father, a relationship which is basically different from that of other men?

Third, Jesus never spoke of the Servant of God. Yet he suffered to an extent that went beyond everything expected before, dying in total solitude without admiring sympathizers who could continue his work. (See chapter 3 [c].) Who is this man? Obviously, a harmless Jesus, a mere prophet or teacher or moral example, will not suffice. Either he was a case of religious mania, living in illusions and dreams of being the incarnation of God's sovereignty on earth, or he was exactly this. However, if he *was* exactly this, we must also say that he *is* exactly this. Is he?

(d) Death and Resurrection—Disclosure of Jesus' Significance

It was only in the crucifixion of Jesus that his rejection by men became universal. Even the innermost circle of his disciples failed; some women were more courageous, but even they were "looking on from afar" and later on went merely in search of a dead body. Thus, faith had come to an end everywhere. It was in this situation that the disciples experienced the presence of the living Lord,

---

[17]In a prayer: Lk 10:21 twice; 11:2; 22:42 (Mt 26:39, 42,); 23:34, 46; cf. John 11:41; 12:27, 28; 17:1-26.

[18]Gottlob Schrenk, "πατήρ," *Theological Dictionary of the New Testament*, 10 vols., ed. Gerhard Friedrich, trans. Geoffrey Bromiley (Grand Rapids: William B. Eerdmans, 1964-1976) 5:981-82, 979n212.

initially in various encounters of Jesus with female and male disciples, some of whom he installed as apostles, and then generally in the coming of the Holy Spirit.

This presence was not the presence of Plato in his philosophy or of Shakespeare in his plays. It did not merely provide the disciples with new knowledge and new feelings; it did not merely enable them to find a new attitude to life and death. All the reports of the New Testament leave no doubt that the risen Lord was identified with Jesus of Nazareth, and the discovery of this identity was an essential part of the post-Easter appearances of Jesus. This is so important because the encounter with the very Jesus whom they had betrayed became for them the liberation of their guilt, not merely for their sense of guilt, but from guilt itself. They understood well enough what it meant that the one whom they had left in Gethsemane came again to them, open, forgiving, even calling them to much greater responsibility than ever before. Thus, faith that was given them again was unmistakably experienced as an unmerited gift.

This meant that the earthly ministry of Jesus was certainly not forgotten. On the contrary, only after the resurrection was its real significance understood for the disciples now experienced what had happened when Jesus invited a tax collector to his table or allowed a prostitute to anoint him. Only now did the disciples detect how much this was the decisive event in all the words and deeds of Jesus because on Good Friday guilt had become universal. Whether spoken and done to those that were considered outsiders or to those who were considered insiders of the chosen people of God, or even to the group of the disciples nearest to him, all the words and deeds of Jesus were vehicles of that unbelievable grace of God, which accepted those who rejectd him and embraced them in a stream of love that made them become children of God. Without this experience words like "grace," "forgiveness," or even "messiah" would remain words of a foreign and unknown language.

This answers two questions about the nature of revelation. First, why did Jesus never clearly and unmistakably proclaim himself as the messiah or the Son of God or the servant of God? His avoidance of all well-known titles or definitions reflects the same basic approach manifested in his preference for parabolic language as opposed to direct language. As he did not provide his hearers with new information about God or the Spirit or sin or forgiveness, knowledge that they could simply accept and take home to possess forever, neither did he give them a title by which they could in some way capture him and dispose of him. If he had revealed himself as the messiah, everybody would have had a different picture of what the messiah should be: a national hero, a teacher of the law, a heavenly redeemer changing the earth into a paradise, and so on. It is, perhaps, comparable to what happens when I go to a party. Let us assume that I meet there a man who has had bad experiences with pastors. If he knows that I am a pastor, he perceives me according to his preconceived stereotype of a pastor: I am just a hypocrite, preaching what I do not believe myself, while enjoying my easy and profitable job. I may be able to correct that idea but I have to fight against it all evening long, and I am not able to speak about what is in my heart. Even if my acquaintance had a more positive picture of a pastor, the situation would be basically the same. He would perceive me according to that ideal and illusionary picture of a pastor he had previously formulated and would not meet the real me until after I succeeded in correcting his sterotype of me. Let us now assume that he does not know my profession. Then I am free to discuss with him that about which I am deeply concerned, and we may understand each other better and better. After hours of good dialogue he may ask about my profession and the next morning he may say to a friend, "I tell you, this John Smith is really a pastor!" Then, as a result of this experience, "pastor" has a totally new meaning for him. This is exactly what happened when after the resurrection the church said, "We tell you, this Jesus of Nazareth really is the Christ."

The problem, then, is not the well-known question of whether Jesus thought of himself as the messiah, if "messiah" means a figure within a given pattern that serves to describe, explain, and understand him. When members of the early church confessed "Jesus—Christ" it did not mean that they knew in advance what the term "Christ" meant and then attached it to Jesus because he fulfilled all the qualifications of that title. It meant rather that in the ministry of Jesus, most of all in his death and his resurrection, they had come to understand for the first time what this term "Christ" really means.

This provides the answer to the second question: Why are the Christologies in the New Testament (that is, the titles, the formulae, the hymns, and the systems by which disciples and apostles and other believers tried to proclaim Jesus as the Christ) so very different from one another and at times even contradictory? We have seen that a term like "grace" or "messiah" does not really help one to understand Jesus rightly without the experience of the one who uses it. Of course the term conveys a certain idea to anybody. For instance, "messiah" designates one in whom God's decisive and final salvation becomes a reality. But again words like "decisive," "final," "salvation," and even "God" can only describe the "non plus ultra," the unsurpassable quality of that figure, and may not flesh out the linguistic skeleton with a communicable reality. Such terms always reflect quite a spectrum within which the experience of the hearer may be wakened to real understanding.

Therefore, understanding the New Testament is like drinking water. A mountaineer knows that water flowing directly from melting snow does not help because "pure" water, as we can distill it, does not quench the thirst. Water must contain minerals from the soil—perhaps even some mud (of course, not too much!)—to quench my thirst. Therefore, a pure confession is impossible. It must contain something of the soil in which it originated, and it would be wrong to try to purify it. We may, to a certain degree, substitute the mud of Palestine in the first century A.D. for that of America in the twentieth century. We may remove some of the excess mud that hides rather than reveals the truth, but we can never distill it to a pure truth with a timeless correctness.

(e) "I am the Resurrection and the Life"

The words of John 11:21-28 express clearly what I want to say. While this passage does not repeat literally what Jesus spoke, it may convey to us his meaning in terms of our post-Easter understanding better perhaps than sayings of Jesus himself, his "ipissima verba." It is the dialogue between Jesus and Martha after the death of her brother Lazarus. Martha starts with an "if": "Lord, if you had been here, my brother would not have died," exactly as we often start: "If I had not fallen ill . . . if I had only been allowed to go to the university . . . if I had married that girl. . . ." Of course, none of these "ifs" are expressive of reality. Therefore, we remain in a kind of retrospective posture or stance that leads nowhere. Martha, however, is a faithful, believing Jew. Hence she goes on: "And even now I know that whatever you ask from God, God will give you." She believes this honestly; and yet, when Jesus says his next sentence, it becomes clear that in reality she does not reckon with the possibility that this could really happen here and now. "Jesus says to her: 'Your brother will rise again.' " There it is, the promise of an unbelievable miracle. And "Martha said to him: 'I know that he will rise again in the resurrection at the last day.' " Thus she relegates the reality of that promise to the faraway last day. This is typical of our way of believing. She does not doubt, the promise is a reality to her, but a reality in another world "on a religious plane." Nonetheless she can say "I know," and we may envy her this certainty. From where did she get this knowledge? Perhaps from her parents who told her this, or from her friends who share this view, or from her teacher in religion who taught her the doctrine of resurrection. Obviously, she was born in an orthodox family, had grown up in orthodox surroundings, and had been taught by an orthodox Pharisee, not a Sadducee who would have instructed her just the opposite way. Is this the basis of faith in the resurrection, that everybody says it is so and nobody opposes that belief? In this case it would become more and more difficult to believe today.

Now we should not cast away the good with the bad—the baby with the bathwater. We must certainly be grateful to those who have handed down their faith to us. Yet this cannot be the real basis for our faith, a basis strong enough to carry through all distress and temptation. "Jesus said to her: '*I* am the resurrection and the life.' " Martha is not asked about what she knows, about all the creedal statements that she can accept and confess. She is only asked whether she can see in Jesus, who is standing before her, the power of the resurrection and the life which will flow to her and maybe even to Lazarus. The question is no longer whether she believes in a miraculous event at the end of time, at the last day. Orthodoxy could even prevent her from an experience that was not foreseen in the pattern of the creed, while open doubts might enable a person to be open to unexpected experiences. Whether she is an orthodox Jew or full of doubts or even an outsider is not of first importance now. All that is important is whether the word of Jesus leads to a disclosure, whether the resurrection and life of which the creed speaks and anticipates in a faraway future come to life now in her dialogue with Jesus. If this happens then the life of another dimension enters the existence of Martha: "Whoever lives and believes in me shall never die." *The* life, God's life, cannot die, and if it really enters the earthly life of Martha, it becomes part of her. It becomes unmistakably God's life as it is living in *Martha;* in nobody else can it exist in just this way. This life in its specific "Marthan" realization will not and cannot die. Sure Martha will die: "He who believes in me, though he die, yet shall he live." Martha is to die, with her toothaches, with her inferiority—or superiority—complexes, with all of her conscious or unconscious psychic turmoil. It would be dreadful if she could not die. But there is another Martha, created by the word of Jesus, into whom the life of God has entered, and this Martha will live though her earthly body and soul will die.

Jesus asks her: "Do you believe this?" She shows that she has understood: "She said to him: 'Yes, Lord, I believe . . . ' "—not "this" as if it were just an additional point of the creed in which she has been instructed—" 'I believe that you are the Christ, the Son of God, he who is coming into the world.' " She has realized that she has not simply accepted a new dogma but that a new communication has taken place, which has brought her into a new relationship with God. Jesus has come to her and with him God himself, his resurrection and life. She believes, not in a new statement, but in "the one who is coming into the world." And her actions show even better than her words how well she has understood. She does not sit down reflecting on her blindness and sin and the wonderful conversion, which has made her a newborn child of God. She does not focus upon herself, either on her admirable rebirth as a Pharisee would do, or on her sin as a Protestant trained since the Reformation to see himself as a sinner would do. Both would be basically the same, by the way, as it would be the same whether an eddy in a river draws us down and drowns us clockwise or conversely. Martha is cured of all this focus on herself, her sinful or pious ego: "When she had said this, she went and called her sister, saying quietly"—again not "this" or "that" but " 'The Teacher is here and is calling for you.' "

There will be a day on which Martha's physical existence will come to an end. Who will she then be? Will she be her physical body that will be dissolved in a short time? Will she be the person about whom the rabbi (or the priest or the minister) tries to give a portrayal at the funeral? We know how incomplete and often wrong these representations are. Will she be the one who lives on in the memory of her friends and her family? This may come closer to the truth, and yet how little do we know about ourselves, let alone about others! Even in a very good marriage we detect sometimes, after fifty years, actions or reactions that we should never have expected (and this, by the way, is the salt that keeps marriage from becoming tedious). Who will Martha then be? I think she will be what God has begun in her—that new person that he has created in her, now freed from all the many things that have hidden and buried God's work during her earthly life, so that all the fragments are now brought to perfection by the same God who has begun to build them up.

This means: If ever we have *known* that a prayer of ours has been heard, perhaps not fulfilled as we had hoped, but heard; if ever a word of God has really hit us, challenged us, warned us, consoled us, so that we have *known* that it was God who has spoken to us; if ever we have *known* that what has happened in the last days or weeks or months was not simply chance or the effect of human will and action, but was guided by somebody else, and if all this had happened to us only once in our life, then something of that life of another dimension, of that life of God has entered our earthly life and will never die. Then the living Lord has become the resurrection and the life within our physical existence.

I have dealt with this Johannine pericope at some length because I think it points directly to the solution to our problem: In what way shall we understand the earliest Christian confession "Jesus—Christ"? How do we identify a human person living in the Palestine of the first century with God in his presence both to the people of that time and place and the people of the twentieth century in America? The story starts, as it always does, with a specific worldly experience. In Martha's case it begins with the death of a beloved person. Her affliction is met by the kerygma of the resurrection. This leads, first, to a conventional conviction of the reality of a future event: the resurrection at the last day. She accepts this conviction because other persons who have believed in it have taught her of it, and it is supported by the personal encouragement that Jesus' words give her. The implication of this future event may console her, to a certain degree, even in the present. The next step is the Christianization of that general belief: " *I* am the resurrection and the life." This means, first, that the terms "resurrection" and "life" do not remain indefinite descriptions of a future good, but receive some more definite colours. The future life of the resurrection will be, in some essential way, similar to the life of Jesus Christ. However, it is possible that even this knowledge may be objective and remain outside the person who has this knowledge. The main point in the story of John 11 is, second, the fact that the one who says "I am the resurrection and the life" is present to Martha. Therefore, the "I" in this statement is a concrete person with specific traits known to the hearer. This changes the quality of Martha's belief; it becomes faith because the kerygmatic statement of Jesus connects the experience of meeting Jesus, of speaking and listening to him, directly with the truth that it conveys. What we call "disclosure" occurs.

Thus, faith arises when the truth about God is preached into the specific situation of a person. Since God is not merely some highest power but the one who acts in Jesus in a specific and revealing way, it is impossible to understand this truth about God without some reference to the earthly Jesus. On this level one could still discuss whether Bultmann's minimum, the mere fact of Jesus' crucifixion, would not suffice. But if faith is founded on the meeting of the one who said "*I* am the resurrection and the life," if the life, as it is manifest in Jesus' whole ministry, is to become part of our own life, if God cannot remain an object to be observed and perhaps accepted as true, but a dimension of life acting within our existence, then the knowledge of Jesus of Nazareth and of the life of God living in him becomes indispensable. Without it, we do not know what the kerygma proclaims.

Therefore, it is only the kerygma that points to the significance of Jesus not as a human person among others—albeit the highest possible example of a human person—but as the presence of the living God himself. But it is the narrative of the life and death of Jesus and of his encounter with the disciples after Easter that enables us to understand how this living God enters our human and mortal lives, and, thus, makes it possible for us to really understand what the kerygma says. No doubt this may also help us to reformulate the kerygma in our terms so that the step from the kerygma of the New Testament back to the narratives of Jesus and from there again to the kerygma in our modern terms repeats itself time and again. This is especially true since all the narratives are in and of themselves also kerygma because all their authors (at least within the canonical gospels) were convinced of the need to narrate the deeds and words of the crucified and risen Christ. As Edward Schillebeekx writes, "A perpetual movement of the pendulum between the biblical interpretation of Jesus and the interpretation of our experiences of today is essential." [19] We may add that in both of these interpretations a perpetual movement of the pendulum between the kerygma of the earliest and/or the modern church on the one hand and what we know of the earthly Jesus from the biblical reports and/or modern scholarship on the other is essential. What I want to emphasize is that a Jesus of Nazareth who is not seen in the sense of the post-Easter kerygma as the Christ of God is not Jesus of Nazareth at all.

---

[19]Edward Schillebeeckx, *Christus und die Christen, Die Geschichte einer neuen Lebenspraxis* (Freiburg: Herder, 1980) 69.

Chapter 5

EN ROUTE
WITH MY TEACHERS

This autobiographical essay presents a very personal approach to the theological problem with which I have dealt in the Sizemore lectures. There is no doubt about the rather subjective character of my attempt to understand theology in the light of my own development, and to write of this development is only defensible on two accounts. On the one hand, the path I have trod is in many respects similar to that of many other colleagues, some of whom have contributed much more than I to the progress of theological thought. Thus, my experience may be representative of that of many others. On the other hand, any attempt towards the solution of a theological problem is hardly understandable apart from an awareness of the struggle that finally gave rise to the suggestions offered to the reader.

I have been asked many times in the United States why I decided to study theology; European students are usually much too inhibited to ask such intimate and central questions. Thus, I suppose that I should begin with some consideration of this question. As far as I can determine, there was no specific interest in the study of theology among my ancestors. At least as far back as the sixteenth century my forebears were farmers or "surgeons" (which meant that they were able to cup and, perhaps, to suture up a wound), and later on real physicians or lawyers (as was my father), and my parents certainly did not expect me to go into the ministry. Thus, I cannot say why the religious instruction given by our faithful but not extraordinary pastor during the three years before my confirmation interested me so much except, perhaps, for some experiences of answered prayers amidst the troubles of adolescence. I can say, however, that after my confirmation a young chaplain (the leader of a Christian youth group for sixteen- to twenty-year-old boys) was of some influence when at the age of eighteen, I had to decide whether to learn Hebrew in high school as a preparation for theological studies at the university. This young chaplain was going through a very difficult time. His bride had left him, and while we were not aware of this, we could feel the pain with which he was living. At the same time we were aware of a power that sustained him. In short, without any real knowledge of the circumstances or any explanation on his part, and without any demonstration of spectacular heroism or unambiguous proof of God's help, we experienced in him the reality of a life with God. If I had not been able to tell him many years later that this time had been, among other experiences, decisive for my decision to become a minister of the church, he might never have known the significant impact of the witness of his life during those difficult days.

(a) Rudolf Bultmann

After one semester of exposure to the old liberalism with the theological faculty of my native town of Basel in Switzerland, I went to study at Marburg, Germany. I did so because of my interest in the comparative history of religions, an interest about which I shall have more to say in succeeding pages. There I met Rudolf Bultmann, and it was that meeting that decided my destiny. From him I learned, as I mentioned in chapter 1, that the word of God can only be understood existentially. It is not a doctrine that can be heard and accepted in the way that other information can be heard and accepted. It cannot be approached in a neutral, more or less detached way, viewed critically, and then accepted or rejected after weighing the pros and cons. The word of God always has the character of an appeal that touches the very existence of a person and wants to alter it. As a word of love alters my life whether it is answered in an enthusiastic return of love, received in deep gratitude or spurned, so the word of God changes my life (or better: my understanding of life and by this my life itself).

This did not mean that the lecture hall at Marburg University became a revival meeting in which conversions happened continually as the biblical text was being interpreted. Bultmann's very critical mind interpreted the text in as scholarly a way as any of his colleagues might have been able to do. But he interpreted it so that its meaning for human existence became clear. Whether it touched the student personally or not was another question. Even for a person totally open to the message of the gospel there are times when different parts of the text speak to his or her specific situation in different ways. Nonetheless, it became clear to all of Bultmann's students that reading the New Testament was only fruitful and meaningful when the reader was open to the risk of being touched and impacted at the very center of his or her life by the text.

Thus, it is understandable that Rudolf Bultmann was one of the very few theologians who already in the early 1920s had basically understood and accepted Karl Barth's thesis that Jesus was, as the Christ of God, "the level unknown to us . . . cutting vertically from above through the level known to us."[1] Most of his contemporaries were extremely bewildered by the fact that such a liberal and critical scholar as Bultmann could share this new "dialectic" the-

---

[1]Karl Barth, *Der Römerbrief*, 3rd ed. (Munich: Kaiser-Verlag, 1922) 6, cf. also xix. For a bibliography of my own works, see *Die Mitte des Neuen Testaments. Einheit und Vielfalt neutestamentlicher Theologie* [Festschrift für Eduard Schweizer], ed. Ulrich Luz and Hans Weder (Göttingen: Vandenhoeck und Ruprecht, 1983) 427-37.

ology which put the full Christological confession at the center of its understanding of the New Testament. Thus, I was very lucky to learn in the earliest stage of my studies, in my first academic introduction to the New Testament, that a presentation of the gospel in which Jesus was no more than a revered teacher or a moral example was too harmless to challenge the world of today. And I learned this without being forced to give up the freedom of critical scholarship. On the contrary, I was taught not to fear the truth and never to be anxious about detecting something that seemed to endanger my faith since God was always on the side of truth and not illusion.

Bultmann had certainly spent much of his time and strength investigating the "historical Jesus" and trying to distinguish between authentic and inauthentic sayings of or stories about the earthly Jesus. We read his book about Jesus and analyzed the synoptic gospels with the methods presented in his imposing work on *The History of the Synoptic Tradition*. The results of these studies could not shatter our faith; they could only help us to understand even better what the post-Easter proclamation of Jesus as the Christ of God meant. As I emphasized in chapter 1, even if the words and deeds of Jesus had never included an "implicit Christology" (which, according to Bultmann, they did!), it would not change in the slightest way the fact that he really was and is the Christ, the source of all salvation. Thus, the freedom to investigate the truth without fear of the results of such investigation combined with the conviction that the central content of the preaching of the gospel was from the beginning in the New Testament that Jesus was the Christ were Bultmann's invaluable contributions to me as a young student.

(b) The Confessing Church in Germany—Schrenk and Brunner

While still a student I also learned something of the "existential" interpretation of the gospel in a very different way, this time in direct relation to the social and political realities of that time. At the end of my second semester of study in the winter of 1932-1933, I participated in a week of social studies in Berlin led by G. Wünsch, an enthusiastic socialist on the left wing of the party fighting for the rights of the working class. During this week, not far away from the youth hostel in which we were staying, the "Reichstag," the German parliament building, burned down. Hitler, whose own party was responsible, accused the communists of arson and took political power very soon after that. Thus, when I came back to Marburg in my fifth and sixth semesters, Germany was dominated by National Socialism, and nobody could tolerate the illusion of a lecture on ancient texts that did not relate the significance of such texts to contemporary events. Every insight into the meaning of the New Testament texts was full of implications for the practical life of the church and, therefore, also of my German fellow students. Wünsch had shifted to National Socialism and was dominating the faculty; Bultmann, who was of a rather conservative and reluctant character politically, found himself together with his friend, church historian and New Testament scholar Hans von Soden, in the front line in the battle against the "Arierparagraph" (the law that degraded and outlawed the non-Aryan people, especially the Jews, who even when baptized were no longer allowed to share the divine service with their Aryan brothers and sisters).

It was God's special gift to me that I was allowed to study in a period in which it was impossible to separate academic studies from the life of the church and of the world as a whole. To be sure, as a Swiss I was never in real danger, compared with my German friends whose actions or even contributions to a discussion could land them in prison or even in a concentration camp. This threat did not mean, however, that we neglected academic pursuits. On the contrary, we focused all the tools of academic research excessively and eagerly with some special emphasis on Reformation theology. (I read as a student the whole of Calvin's *Institutes* in Latin and most of the New Testament commentaries of Luther and Calvin). We did so because we knew that the better we understood our text grammatically, historically, and systematically, the clearer its meaning for the church would become. Some of my friends read the New Testament so well and so thoroughly that they suffered or even died under Hitler's regime.

When I came to Zurich in my seventh semester, Gottlob Schrenk, professor of New Testament exegesis and theology and son of the famous German evangelist Elias Schrenk, provided something of a counterbalance to Bultmann. Like Bultmann he was open to a critical approach and much interested in Christology as the very center of the New Testament; but whereas Bultmann was mainly influenced by his Lutheran tradition, Schrenk was deeply rooted in the traditions of the Reformed Church. This meant that Schrenk's interest in salvation-history, in the acting of God that precedes man's faith, was always connected with an interpretation directed to the "existence" of the reader and of the church, and it was this that dominated his lectures and seminars.

Emil Brunner, then at the height of his career, was the actual leader of the so-called "Oxford Group movement," a strong movement among lay people, especially business and political leaders, who were learning to listen to God and to live in a responsible Christian way in all their practical decisions. I learned from him how to "translate" (which means literally "to bring over") the message of the New Testament into the life of the church and of the world of business or politics. In Switzerland the danger of Germany's National socialism and the threat it posed was not yet the center of attention. This came later during World War II when I was minister in a village in the Swiss mountains near Zwingli's birthplace. In those days Switzerland was totally surrounded by the German and Italian armies, and nobody could tell when or whether they would invade our country. Already in the summer of 1935 some of Emil Brunner's friends had prepared an intellectual and spiritual defense against the propaganda of the Nazis, but the attention of most people was focused on discerning the impact of the New Testament message for the many decisions necessary in business and politics, and beyond this, for the basic understanding of the structures of our state, our economy and our social responsibility. Even now, fifty years later, there are still people around who learned during these days, especially from Brunner's Bible studies and lectures, how to live and how to act as responsible Christians.

(c) Rudolf Otto

Together with Bultmann and Barth, Emil Brunner was a representative of "dialectical theology." However, the dissolution of that movement was already much in evidence. In 1934 Barth had published his *Nein! (No!)* accusing Brunner of teaching an unorthodox "natural theology" instead of sticking to the word of God alone. In the summer of 1935 we spent hours discussing whether Barth or Brunner or Bultmann was right and why. It was such a fruitful time because all of us, regardless of who our teacher had been, had a common theological perspective: we were convinced that a Christology that acknowledged Jesus Christ as the only hope and salvation for humankind was the center of the New Testament and, therefore, also the central focus of the preaching of the church. We were looking forward to the ministry because we were absolutely convinced that we had come from the darkness of the reign of liberalism to the light of a more correct understanding of the Bible, and we were convinced of the extreme importance of such an understanding for the church and for the social and political world beyond the church. But there were real problems.

I have mentioned how my interest in a comparative history of religions led me first to Marburg. There, along with Bultmann, I encountered Rudolf Otto, the grand old man of religious phenomenology. His book, *Das Heilige (The Holy*, in the sense of a neuter), was a real bestseller. By this time Otto was retired and lectured no more, but he continued to lead a seminar for those who were able to read Sanskrit. In order to participate I learned that language during my third and fourth semesters in Basel. I shall never forget the kindness of that very famous Sanskritist professor Wackernagel to the handful of young students trying to translate those difficult old Iranian texts. "What an interesting translation, Herr Schweizer, but would you not rather prefer to understand it in this way? . . . " was all he said when our attempts to get to the meaning of a difficult sentence were hopelessly wrong!

During my fifth and sixth semesters I was accepted into the small circle of those who read *Bhagavadgita* and *Rigveda* with Rudolf Otto, and it was tempting to detect God's revelation in all religions since the "terrifying" and, at the same time, "fascinating" experience of meeting the world of the "holy" was a phenomenon to be found everywhere, though with different intensity and clarity. For our Western minds at least, it was nowhere to be detected in a clearer and more revealing way than in the prophets of the Old Testament and in the Jesus of the New Testament. In Jesus the neuter "holy" had become the personal "holy one." And yet it was fundamentally the same experience as that of the authors of the *Bhagavadgita* and many other people, known and unknown, in and outside the Jewish/Christian tradition. It was not necessary to discuss whether that dimension of the "holy" was better expressed for an Eastern mind in some form of Buddhism, or for an African mind in some of his legends about the ancestors or in his magical experiences. Otto's perspective allowed for a view that could accept all religions and found one and the same holy God behind the different experiences therein. Whatever their cultural background and religious ideas might be, the same experience of being "terrified and fascinated" by a holy world that lies beyond our rational world belongs to the very structure of human beings.

Personally I found myself returning more and more to the "simple" word of God as found in the Old and the New Testament. Because I had really felt the temptation of Rudolf Otto's enormous knowledge of religions and of his extremely broad approach to them, I was more and more taken by the unpretentious style of the biblical stories or sayings, which were understandable to the simplest minds and at the same time challenging to those of high intelligence. Because I had taken seriously Otto's solution and the texts to which he introduced us, I could return to the Old and New Testament and side definitively with them. However, my studies with Otto made me sensitive to the problems that continued to surface among that group of dialectical theologians that included Bultmann, Brunner and Barth.

Otto's approach was certainly very different from the theology of the word of God that we heard in the lectures of Bultmann. During those days Otto suffered severely when he realized how Bultmann's insistence on the "kerygma" as found in the New Testament, especially in Paul and John, attracted the students. The revival of Luther's doctrine of justification by faith rather than works in Bultmann's theology would not give a central place to religion as a human means of seeking and finding God. The word of God, the kerygma of the church, was the gift of God, not simply the result of human philosophical or ethical efforts. Would it not be logical to see religion as a human attitude on the side of the "works of the law" rather than that of the "mere gift of grace?" And yet, Bultmann did have a central interest in the human answer to the word. He saw the *Vorverständnis*, the preliminary knowledge of God, man's impulse to reflect upon himself, to ask about the meaning of his life, to go beyond the visible and rationally accessible world, as belonging to the very structure of human beings (see chapter 1[c]). It is, therefore, to be found in all religions and philosophies, though Bultmann argued that it is only the proclamation of the New Testament church that brings the full knowledge of the God who justifies the sinner. This certainly differed from Rudolf Otto's view. For Bultmann all presentiments of a divine and holy being were only *Vorverständnis*, hints to the answer to be found in the word of the church, the center of which was justification by grace. But Otto also wanted to see Jesus as the summit of all experiences of a "holy" world, though he would have concentrated on the earthly Jesus rather than on the Christology of Paul and John.

More important—to me at least—was the relationship between the thought of the two Marburg giants at another point. When asked why one should accept the preaching of the church (or a philosophy of justification by grace) and what would convince him of this new biblical understanding of existence, Bultmann would have pointed to Jesus himself. He was the one who had embodied this view in his life and death in a way that became and will become time and again infectious to his disciples. At this point, as far as the meaning of the earthly Jesus was concerned, we were back to the categories of example and imitation. It was not Otto's general experience of a terrifying and fascinating holy power everywhere on earth nor was it the moral example to be followed by man's willing decision to imitate it, but rather the insight into the total givenness of human existence personified in Jesus that would convince the believer. Nonetheless, the concentration on the human experience of God and the parallelism of the experience of Jesus with that of his followers played a central role for Bultmann. Is Bultmann's understanding of Jesus as first of all the motivation (see chapter 1[a]) so far away from Otto's idea of man being "caught" by the experiences of a "holy" power to be detected best in Jesus' life and preaching? These were the problems that lay unsolved and still in disorder in my mind when I came to Karl Barth.

(d) Karl Barth

In my eighth and last semester, Karl Barth, having just been expelled from Germany, taught in Basel. His special seminar of only four students met in his home. Our turn to sit in one of the easy chairs came every fortnight. During that term Barth asked me to tell him about Bultmann's view of justification by grace and not by works, a view that had been very helpful to me up to that time. For a whole evening I presented and defended what I had learned, while Barth restricted himself to raising questions aimed at a better understanding of Bultmann's thesis. The next week Barth argued his own position over against Bultmann, and in so doing helped me to a certain breakthrough. Perhaps this breakthrough might be best expressed by means of a fictitious anecdote. Suppose one were to ask Bultmann when he had been converted. In his response Bultmann would first have altered the terminology, preferring to speak of having changed his understanding of his existence (which seems to be about the same thing). He would also probably have insisted that this had to happen time and time again. Finally, he would have pointed to the time when he had understood for the first time the doctrine of justification by faith, an understanding which had changed his life definitively. (He might, for instance, have pointed to his first lecture on Martin Luther's exposition of Romans.) It is in that new understanding of man's existence as a gift of grace, not to be achieved by his own works, that man finds his salvation.

Barth, on the other hand, would have answered the same question much as one of his spiritual predecessors, Hermann Friedrich Kohlbrugge (a Reformed pastor and author in Elberfeld, who lived from 1803-1875) had: "On Good Friday, A.D. 30" (or whenever Jesus had been crucified). When, in 1950, I tried to describe Bultmann's theology as objectively as possible, I contrasted it to Barth's view. Siding with Barth, I compared the message of the New Testament to an act of grace liberating the incarcerated. Legally, the incarcerated man is free the moment this act of grace takes place. However, until he hears of his liberation and believes it to be a reality, his situation remains unchanged until the day on which he is actually led out of the prison (in biblical terms: up to the day on which "we shall see the Lord as he is," 1 Jn 3:2); however, once he believes the message of his liberation, his situation is totally changed, even while he still sits in the prison.[2]

This did not, of course, solve the problem of other religions, a problem with which I am still wrestling. I could never agree totally with Barth's answer, logical as it was. For him religion, whether Christian or non-Christian, belongs to the realm of humanity's futile efforts to effect an encounter with God. It is part of humanity's ill-fated attempt to ascend to heaven, and ultimately is a reflection of human sin. But neither did Bultmann's "preunderstanding" nor Brunner's natural theology suffice, right as either might be. Perhaps the answer is more simple yet. If God's act of grace is the really decisive factor, if it is he who "is at work in us, both to will and to work for his good pleasure" (Phil 2:13), even when we answer him in faith, if it is the vine itself that creates the fruit of the branches (Jn 15:4), if the seed does sprout and grow, its sower not knowing how (Mk 4:27), would it not be right to say that God looks with mercy on all our activities and that he blesses them and makes them fruitful by his grace whenever and wherever it pleases him? Then all our lives of searching for God, of longing after him, of following our presentiments, even of answering his revelation in gratitude, in piety, and in good works are certainly important, but on a secondary level. They are good only when permeated by his grace.

This means that all religious activity, Christian and non-Christian, may be gracefully accepted and blessed by God. Therefore, we need neither judge nor condemn all human religion as sin nor evaluate it too highly as presentiment or as natural piety. When we have learned to know God in Jesus, we shall speak of him gratefully, joyfully and enthusiastically to any who will listen, never thinking that we are necessarily superior to a non-Christian. To put it in the form of a simile: suppose I had known my father for twenty years before my younger brother was born, and that this younger brother had never actually known him. I could never deny that he might be much the better son of the father and that the father might enjoy him much more than me; nonetheless, I shall always be grateful for my experience of the father, and I shall tell my younger brother about the father if and when he wants to know. Thus, though knowing that the Buddhist may be much nearer to God than I, I shall tell him of Jesus, if he is willing to listen, convinced that in Jesus God has turned his very face towards us. This view has developed slowly as the result of many helpful discussions with friends and colleagues.

Let us return now to the time of the end of my studies in Basel. I wrote my dissertation on the (so-called!) Johannine parables between mid-September 1937 and mid-April 1938, after having completed six months of ministry internship with a pastor and having assumed, for nine months, a city parish of 13,500 members in Basel. I owed the topic of my thesis, the statement of the

---

[2]Eduard Schweizer, "Zur Interpretation des Kreuzes bei Rudolf Bultmann" in *Aux sources de la tradition chrétienne* [Festschrift for Maurice Goguel] (Neuchâtel: Delachaux et Niestlé, 1950) 228-38.

problem, and the method by which to tackle it to Rudolf Bultmann. At this time, however, it was virtually impossible to study and to pass examinations in Hitler's Germany. So I brought my finished thesis to K. L. Schmidt in Basel, and he kindly accepted it.[3] As is typical of my work in general, I had no new and brillant ideas. What I discovered, because I had learned under Bultmann to work hard with an almost ascetic discipline and as exactly as possible, was an insight, the importance of which I could hardly have imagined at the time. As a result of my study I realized that sayings like "I am the true vine" were not similes that would merely say that Jesus was something like a vine or bread or a shepherd. They were, in fact, precise statements to be taken seriously in the literal sense of the words. They declared that it is Jesus alone who is, in the deepest sense of this term, "the *true* vine." This was, in many ways, congenial with Bultmann's theology. According to him, Paul had asked where man could find his justification before God if not in his own works, and had answered that it is Jesus alone who is our justification. John had expanded this view and included all possible aspects of man's life and problems (see chapter 3[f]). Man is searching for meat and drink ("bread" and "water"), for illumination about his situation and for leadership ("light" and a "good shepherd"), for acceptance into a community (into the "vine" Israel),[4] and these things are to be found only in Jesus Christ.

What the combined studies of many American and European scholars on the parables of Jesus have unearthed in the past two decades could have been sensed even then. In a very pointed way John insists on the fact that God, as he is revealed in Jesus Christ, is a reality, over against which all our realities, and even more the language with which we speak of them, are but unsatisfying reproductions. The "I" of Jesus is a subject that cannot be defined by any human predicate. It is, instead, just the other way round. Whatever we call "reality" is actually defined by him. Thus, because there is *one* good shepherd, human shepherds of all kind may lead in the right direction and, therefore, become, in a secondary way, good shepherds. If we carry this idea to its logical conclusion, we may say that there are no human words or concepts at all that can adequately describe God, and therefore, God is ultimately not teachable. There is, however, the promise that human beings, who are constantly being deceived and left without help in their search for bread and water, light and life, will experience these realities in Jesus.

(e) The Living Lord in His Church
and in the World of Social and Political Problems

Insights into the very nature of Jesus' proclamation of God in parables and into the limits (or, better, into the new quality) of all human proclamation of God lay still far in the future, though the results of my dissertation should have

---

[3]Eduard Schweizer, *EGO EIMI. Die religionsgeschichtliche Herkunft und theologische Bedeutung der johanneischen Bildreden, zugleich ein Beitrag zur Quellenfrage des vierten Evangeliums*, Forschungen zur Religion und Literatur des Alten und Neuen Testamentes (Göttingen: Vandenhoeck und Ruprecht, 1939; 2nd ed., 1965).

[4]See §g of this chapter and nn. 37 and 38.

led me further in that direction. After a short excursion in the history of the early church for my *Habilitationsschrift* (a second thesis giving one authority to teach within a theological faculty),[5] I spent almost ten years in the parish ministry in Nesslau, a farmers' village in the mountains of the Toggenburg, not too far from St. Gall. During this period I wrote *Das Leben des Herrn in der Gemeinde und ihren Diensten (The Life of the Lord in the Congregation and Its Services)*. This work, published in 1946, was rewritten in 1959 under the title *Gemeinde und Gemeindeordnung im Neuen Testament.*[6] In this work I wanted to emphasize that it is the *Lord* himself who is living in the community; he is living in the *congregation* as a whole, not merely in single pious individuals, and he is living only if and as long as *services* are rendered among the members of the community and to persons outside of the church.

The problem of how the church of Christ should be manifested in the concrete congregation has concerned me throughout my life. No doubt the witness of those who suffered under Hitler for their efforts to manifest in the life of the church something of the life of its Lord was a significant influence on my studies and reflections on this subject. I cannot imagine a faith that would not find its incorporation in togetherness with other people, primarily in the community of those who believe in Christ. Mere imitation of one of the many forms and orders of the church in the New Testament is of no avail. The form and the order of the church must, in the context of a given place and time, be built up from the very center of the gospel as it is to be proclaimed in that place and that time. There is no model that can simply be imitated in all places and times.

One of the most important criteria by which the adequacy of the form and order of the church may be judged is the extent to which every member is taken seriously with his or her gift. This means, for example, that though the deacon or the Sunday school teacher or the invalid who renders the service of intercession does not act in the same way as the pastor, they are nevertheless to be taken as seriously as the pastor. This basic equality of all services rendered to the honor of God should be expressed as clearly as possible in the church's rites of institution, installation, or ordination, in the way people are incorporated into the Sunday or weekday services, and even in the way they are paid. This means that we should cultivate our fantasy to invent ever new occasions for common actions and discussions, for delegated responsibilities, for visits between different groups, and for reports of their experiences to the whole congregation, and by all this to overcome the isolation of the ministry of the pastor. This is not to minimize the importance, the seriousness, and the glory of the specific ministry of the one who is allowed to spend four years exclusively in the study of the Scripture and is given the freedom to serve under and for the Word of

---

[5]Eduard Schweizer, "Diodor von Tarsus als Exeget," *Zeitschrift für die neutestamentliche Wissenschaft* 40 (1941): 33-75.

[6]See Eduard Schweizer, *Church Order in the New Testament* (London: SCM Press, 1961, 1963, 1979).

God for his or her whole life. It is only to underline the fact that such a ministry can only be fruitful in the context of the living congregation.

Many people sensed in Bultmann's theology the danger of a dissipation of real history into a timeless consciousness of existence that would become more and more introspective and contemplative.[7] My interest in how a church orders itself in its concrete life in the here and now may be understood as an effort to counteract this danger. To a much greater extent this is true of the emphasis on the social and political dimension of the gospel that has developed in the USA and Europe and still more in Latin America and Africa. There is no doubt that Bultmann always knew and emphasized that the gift of justification was, by necessity, to be embodied in the love that serves one's fellow human beings wherever and whenever they are in need. Of course, such a response will include not only the giving of alms, but also an involvement in the struggle for social and political justice and for the human rights of any minority. His protest of discrimination against non-Aryan church members demonstrated this clearly. I can see no other basis for the social and/or political activity of the church within or beyond its own walls. I see this dimension of the life of the church in a much more significant way today than I did in the 1950's, and I have certainly learned to be more grateful for what people outside of the church have taught me by their exemplary actions and by their appeals, propositions and publications. But at that time I tried to get beyond Bultmann's theology at another point. I tried to see all ethical action of the church, be it on an individual, social or political level, as "the life of the Lord," as his own gift to his church. That means that I tried to understand every achievement in this area as intensely as possible, as the result of the merciful acts of God towards his church.

It was about this time that Karl Barth was trying to establish an analogy between God's order of salvation on the one hand and the order of the civil community on the other. I was skeptical of such a direct parallelism of the "City of God" and the secular city. There are no doubt some guiding principles from God's order of salvation which should be applied. It is certainly not God's will that the rich become richer and richer while the poor become poorer and poorer. Hence the church has to fight resolutely against any social and political order that leads to that result. Thus, as far as the general evaluation of goals, there is no choice; but as to how those goals are to be reached, there are alternatives. In some instances, for example, the question of how to build up a community in which justice is done to all of its members, among people who do not know experiences of the grace of God to which one could appeal, is often a question of political reason and common sense. Should the state be basically liberal, fostering a free enterprise economy, which is restricted by laws aimed at the protection of the socially deprived? Or should the state be basically socialist, fostering state-controlled means of production, which is restricted by laws that

---

[7]Fernando Belo, *Das Markusevangelium materialistisch gelesen* (Stuttgart: Alektor, 1980) 353-54.

guarantee human rights and freedom? Should the church in a given situation fight for reforms and laws that counterbalance the general tendency of the state whenever and wherever it becomes dangerous? Should it become a revolutionary group or call its members to participate in such groups? All these questions must be answered time and time again, and they must always be answered according to the contemporary context. Error will be unavoidable, but error is not unbelief. Disputes and conflicts are possible within the same church; they are to be expected. While it is possible to call a fellow Christian names, even to call him an idiot who has forsaken every vestige of sound reason, one should not call him or her an unbeliever, a non-Christian. There is a basic difference between the questions of foundation that are to be answered unambiguously on the one hand, and tactical questions of how to succeed in the political arena on the other hand, between the vision common to all Christians and the way to realize it socially and politically. This difference must never be forgotten.

Sometimes different approaches must be employed by different persons, even in the same time and situation. Personally, I think that it was right and in keeping with God's will that the majority of Swiss citizens were ready to fulfill their military service when, in 1940, Hitler threatened to invade Switzerland (and to kill not only many Swiss people but also thousands of refugees who had found some asylum in our country). At the same time, I think that God had called a small minority to refuse any military service even then as a warning to all against all glorification of killing and any form of shallow patriotism that would forget the dreadful nature of war. In a short contribution to this discussion, written in 1975, I pointed to the "ethical pluralism of the New Testament," arguing for a basic openness to diversity within the church with regard to different social and political decisions combined with a basic unity with regard to the general vision of the goal to be reached.[8]

It is one of the gifts given to me and also one of the limits enjoined on me that the concept (or rather the concepts) of the church in the New Testament and their importance for the vision of an ecumenical church in today's world became more and more central to my interests. I am certainly aware of the danger of a church that retires into a ghetto, of a bloodless theology speculating in an ivory tower far removed from the social and political realities and the real wants and needs of people. But I am also aware of the danger of identifying the gospel directly with the program of a particular political party, whether it supports the divine right of the emperor or National Socialism or, on the contemporary scene, a leftist or even anarchist vision. Those among us who remember the enthusiasm of the first years under Hitler are skeptical of programs that promise happiness forever—we have had bad experiences with our experiments, as Gerhard Sauter once said. Arguments from both sides of the issue have been published in *Evangelische Theologie* 44/2 (1984) and my own arguments have been taken up in the editor's contribution to the discussion.[9]

---

[8]Eduard Schweizer, "Ethischer Pluralismus im Neuen Testament," *Evangelische Theologie* 35 (1975): 397-401.

[9]See *Evangelische Theologie* 44 (1984): 112-37.

It goes without saying that a disciple of Jesus, living in today's world, is responsible for the social and political life of his country and, perhaps, also of the world beyond the borders of his homeland, and we are to be very grateful to all those within the church who have called us back to this responsibility. However, my interest lies in the specific character of all actions and programs as proposed or achieved by the church or, as it is expressed in the title of my early book, the life of the Lord in all these actions and programs. It also goes without saying that it is often necessary for a member of the church to cooperate in such struggles with people who consider themselves outside of the church. This is certainly not to demean their position in any way since such people have so often put the church to shame. Still, the church will know an ultimate authority that enables it to defend the weak in a world stamped by the law of the survival of the fittest (see chapter 1[b]); it will learn to be confident even in defeat; it will always be critical of its own actions and programs and, therefore, be able to draw the line where it must be drawn with regard to tactical recommendations that are no longer ethically defendable; it will be intolerant of all untrue caricatures of the enemy, because it always sees, even in the adversary, the human being to be won; it will, thus, be very reluctant to judge quickly. Hence, the church's emphasis will always lie in convincing as many as possible of the goodness of its cause, of the necessity of reform, rather than on specific strategies promising a sure victory. The desire of the church is to change the view of its opponents, not to ride roughshod over them.

(f) The Preeminence of Grace and the Human Answer to It

Of greater importance to me was another problem: How are we to describe the preeminence of the gracious action of God over against our believing or doubting reaction, a reaction that follows it in a secondary way and is dependent on the prior action of God himself? How is it possible to find a language faithful to the New Testament message and understandable in our time? Barth had defended the position of Anselm of Canterbury who had argued that the sin of humanity could not simply be set aside by God. It is so serious that justice has to be dispensed; but since atonement could be made only by a sinless one, Jesus Christ is the only one who could do so. I had been taught by Bultmann that Mark 10:45 ("The Son of Man has come not to be served but to serve and to give life as a ransom for many") was probably not an authentic word of Jesus. This view has been contested again recently;[10] nevertheless, this isolated saying would provide a very limited foundation in Jesus' own teaching for a doctrine of atonement in the sense of Anselm. Moreover, the Pauline form of the words of institution in which the cup is not equated with the blood but with the new covenant in the blood seems to be, on the whole, closer to the words of Jesus at that last supper than the Markan form "This is my blood of

---

[10]"Sühne oder Versöhnung?" in *Die Mitte des Neuen Testaments*, 294-95, 308; cf. n. 1 above.

the covenant."[11] Such a conclusion might further support the view that the idea of a ransom to be paid to God to substitute for what we owe him does not seem to go back to Jesus himself. This is not to say that such an idea is wrong; there are, after all, New Testament passages that employ this imagery. It does mean, however, that it should be possible to employ different imagery for the significance of Jesus' death without lowering Jesus to the status of a mere teacher or moral example or motivation for our faith. Jesus, in all probability, could get along without the reflections of Anselm and the language shaped by them. Certainly Paul and John use other images and other ways of speaking to express the central importance of Jesus crucified and risen, and the later literature of the New Testament manifests a plurality of such images and concepts.

My first attempt to address this problem was my book *Erniedrigung und Erhöhung bei Jesus und seinen Nachfolgern (Humiliation and Exaltation with Jesus and His followers)* published 1955. I rewrote it in a much shorter form for the English edition in 1960.[12] When a second edition in German became necessary in 1962, I rewrote the book more or less along the lines of the English version without, however, being forced to shorten it so much (compared with the first German edition). It certainly represents the first step of a beginner, the work of a "learner," and other scholars have taken it up and have, in a more critical and more precise way, proceeded in the same direction.[13] The task that awaited me and my successors, many of whom made a more significant contribution than I, was to find on as broad a basis as possible in the New Testament itself, a model that would express the preeminence of the acts of God in Jesus Christ in a way that would, at the same time, be relatively close to the way Jesus himself taught in his earthly life, faithful to the post-Easter proclamation of Jesus Christ by the church and understandable for people of today. I am still of the opinion that the model of "humiliation and exaltation" is a possible model for such a program. It emphasizes the solidarity of God with humankind in the humiliation of Jesus, up to his death on the cross, as well as the "over against"

---

[11]Eduard Schweizer, *The Lord's Supper According to the New Testament*, Facet Books Biblical Series 18 (Philadelphia: Fortress Press, 1968) 10-17.

[12]See Eduard Schweizer, *Lordship and Discipleship*, Studies in Biblical Theology 28 (London: SCM Press, 1960).

[13]See L. Ruppert, *Der leidende Gerechte. Eine motivgeschichtliche Untersuchung zum Alten Testament und zwischentestamentlichen Judentum*, Forschungen zur Bibel 5 (Würzburg, 1972); Ruppert, *Der leidende Gerechte und seine Feinde. Eine Wortfelduntersuchung* (1973); Ruppert, *Jesus als der leidende Gerechte? Der Weg Jesu im Lichte eines alt- und zwischentestamentlichen Motivs*, Stuttgarter Bibelstudien (Stuttgart, 1972); Karl Theodor Kleinknecht, *Der leidende Gerechtfertigte. Untersuchungen zur alttestamentlich-jüdischen Tradition vom "leidenden Gerechten" und ihrer Rezeption bei Paulus*, Wissenschaftliche Untersuchungen zum Neuen Testament 2. Reihe 13 (Tübingen: J. C. B. Mohr, 1984). Whereas, in the preparation of my article on *pneuma* (spirit) the newly discovered Dead Sea Scrolls had been the most important background, it was now the Old Testament and especially the Wisdom Literature (Wisdom 2:10-5:5).

of the exalted Lord ruling over his church. In the same year (1955) Karl Barth published his study of Christology in his giant Dogmatics and stressed that in Christ God has taken up all humanity with all its successes and failures into his own world; in Jesus' humiliation he has identified with all the ups and downs of man, and in the resurrection he remained faithful to this act, because as our intercessor the exalted Christ brings all our successes and all our shortcomings into the presence of the living God.

When I added "und seinen Nachfolgern" ("and to those that follow him") or "and Discipleship" (in the English title), I did so because I wanted to clarify as much as possible, especially in this first fledgling book on Christology, the character of faith as *a way of living*. Since my studies under Bultmann, I had rejected any view that understood faith as merely an intellectual assent to doctrine and had come to see faith as an event that embraces and permeates the whole of one's existence, the very life of a person. There is no doubt about the importance of clear confessional formulations, of doctrinal statements and their concentration in dogmas. I could never forget this after having witnessed the birth of the Barmen Confession and the enormous importance of crystal clear statements drawing definite lines between right and wrong in the fight of the church against Hitler! The struggle of the Confessing Church in Germany would not have been possible without its confessional formulae. But all these statements and formulations function like the rails along a highway. I cannot get along without the rails because they prevent me from driving to the right into a swamp or to the left over a cliff, and during night time they show me, with their cat's eyes, the direction of the road. However, they are not the road itself, and if I confuse them with the road and try to drive on them, I shall meet with catastrophe in no time. Thus, faith cannot live without dogmatic statements, but it is essentially different from a mere acceptance of them; it has to find its way, to "drive" in between the "rails," and this "driving" requires that we never stay at the same point by the rails, but proceed on the road.

Ten years of ministry in a mountain village, the population of which consisted of about two thousand people, mostly farmers, and, to a much greater degree, also the long and good partnership with my wife, our four children, and ten grandchildren have taught me more and more how much faith expresses itself and lives only in the totality of our existence, in our seeing and sensing and experiencing, in our emotions and unconscious reactions as well as in our thinking. The "mystical" concept of "Dying and Rising with Christ"[14] began to preoccupy me more and more, this idea that the believer is sharing the destiny of his Lord, an experience in which the future fulfillment becomes in some way present because God lets human beings participate in his own act-

---

[14]Eduard Schweizer, "Die 'Mystik' des Sterbens und Auferstehens mit Christus bei Paulus," *Evangelische Theologie* 26 (1966): 239-57; published in English as "Dying and Rising with Christ," *New Testament Studies* 14 (1967-1968): 1-14; also in *New Testament Issues*, ed. Richard Batey (New York: Harper and Row, 1970) 173-90.

ing. It is always a participation of the whole person and never of his thoughts only.

Looking back to what I wrote thirty years ago, I am tempted to think that the most relevant part of that book was to be found in the image on the first page and the fact that I could not deal with the problem adequately except in an image. It is the image of a boy following his father who makes a way through three feet of new snow. The boy steps in the very footprints of his father. He experiences the same cold that his father felt. Yet he does all of this in a totally different way because his father has gone before him and opened the way. He has done for the boy what the boy could not have done. His father is not merely his teacher or his moral example, for the boy does not have to follow along breaking his own way, while only being allowed to ask his father how to do it and then trying to imitate him. But neither is his father merely his substitute. The boy cannot stay at home in the warmth of the living room, believing that his father is going in his place. He also must go. Thus, neither a liberal theology that sees Jesus as teacher and example nor a theology that focuses strictly on a vicarious death in which Jesus becomes our substitute will do. I shall consider further the importance of the language of imagery in the succeeding pages.

(g) The Influence of Hellenistic (Gnostic) Concepts on the New Testament Message

A change in my thinking manifests itself at another point. I started work on my article on πνεῦμα ("spirit") for Kittel's *Theological Dictionary of the New Testament*[15] while professor at the University of Mainz. Those years immediately following World War II were hard years. Mainz was a city bombed to ruins, without heat for the very cold winter, and with almost no food. Still those difficult years were full of adventure, resignation, despair, and hope. I finished the article in my first year at the University of Zurich in 1949-1950. In this, my first contribution to the ten volumes of that massive dictionary, I put the implications of both the newly discovered and as yet unpublished Dead Sea Scrolls and the Gnostic writings at the beginning, before dealing with the New Testament. From Bultmann I had learned a history-of-religions perspective that suggested that the New Testament contained fragments of a myth that existed as a whole only in Gnostic writings. It was suggested that the New Testament concept of a descending and ascending savior was borrowed from Gnostic myth. Actually, the Gnostic writings only presented the imagery in which the New Testament writers conveyed the truth of the call to authentic existence (Bultmann's "Eigentlichkeit") offered by the Christ-event.

Of course, there is no way to speak of God adequately without also speaking of human existence as being determined by him. But, conversely, there is

---

[15]See Eduard Schweizer, "πνεῦμα," in *Theological Dictionary of the New Testament*, 10 vols., ed. Gerhard Friedrich, trans. Geoffrey W. Bromiley (Grand Rapids: William B. Eerdmans, 1964-1976) 6:389-455. See also Schweizer, *The Spirit of God* (London: Adam and Charles Black, 1960).

no way of speaking truly of human existence without speaking of God as being its determining factor. The decisive question, then, is how to relate the one way of speaking to the other, how to decide about the priority of the one statement over against the other. Is it theologically possible to confine discussion to the religious experiences of man, and only later to acknowledge that they are the result of an act of God? Or is it necessary to think and to speak first of God's acts, before thinking and speaking of the human answer to them, in order to define all human reactions as gifts of God's Spirit? Or is this merely a misguided effort to distingush two alternatives that are in reality indistinguishable? To be sure, the historical problem of whether or not a Gnostic myth existed when Paul wrote his letters does not solve these questions. And yet, the time and energy I gave to studying the historical problem of the possible priority of the Gnostic myth demonstrates how much the *systematic* question (which is not actually dependent on the historical facts) had captured my interest—the question of whether or not the narrative of Jesus Christ coming to dwell among human beings and being exalted to his lordship over church and world was mythical imagery borrowed from Gnosticism.

In 1970, while doing research in Hellenistic writings during work on a commentary on the letter to the Colossians, I discovered a pre-Pauline Pythagorean text dating from the first century B.C. (allegedly going back to the fourth century B.C.). The background of this text is not to be found in Gnosticism,[16] but rather in middle Platonism, which experienced a revival about this time and remained strong throughout the New Testament period emphasizing the idea that the soul ascends after physical death and must find its way through the "elements of the world." This phrase is used exclusively to designate the natural elements of earth, water, fire, and air.[17] These are, according to Empedocles, the "four roots of everything that exists."[18] There is constant strife among these elements and this "mighty strife amongst the members" is, according to Aristotle, the principle of transitoriness[19] or, in the words of a contemporary of the author to the Colossians, "the destruction of everything through everything."[20] Therefore, salvation depends on the purity of the soul. If it has purified itself during earthly life by liberating itself more and more from the contact with all the elements of this world, it is light enough to ascend through all four elements to that place above where it will rest for ever in eternal bliss.

---

[16]Hans Diels, *Die Fragmente der Vorsokratiker*, 8th ed., ed. W. Kranz (1956) 1:448-51.

[17]Josef Blinzler, *Lexikalisches zu dem Terminus ta stoicheia tou kosmou bei Paulus*, Analecta Biblica 17-18 (Rome, 1963) 439-41; see also Valentinus as quoted in Irenaeus, *adv. haereses*, 1, 1,10-48.

[18]Diels, *Fragmente* 1, 31(21). For all evidence cf. my essay cited in n23.

[19]Aristotle, *Metaphysics*, 11:4 (1000ab).

[20]Diels, *Fragmente* 1 183:8.

During the first century A.D., Cicero[21] described this process in terms of the natural law of physics. He suggested that as soon as the weight of the soul is the same as that of the ether surrounding it, it swings up and down for a short time and then comes to rest. If, however, the soul is still infected by earthly elements, still bound to the four elements of the world, it will sink, and the elements will capture it again. Thus, the souls of bad people are chased through all the elements, hated by all of them.[22] The same ideas are also found in contemporary Jewish literature, especially in Philo; they are taken up by Plutarchus around A.D. 100 and by the church fathers of the second century. Reference to such a view may be found scattered from Heraclitus in the sixth century B.C. up to the collectors of the sixth century A.D. Evidences of such a view are concentrated in the fragments of the Pythagoreans, but may also be seen in the books of Philo, in some traditions of Jewish rabbis, in Plutarchus (who wrote ten unfortunately lost books on Empedocles), and even in the earliest patristic literature. The zenith of these ideas seems to have been reached from the middle of the first century B.C. to the middle of the second century A.D.[23] The Pythagorean text speaks of the four elements. As long as these elements are balanced over against each other, there is peace in the world, but this world is unstable, unhealthy, mortal. The immortal souls are guided above into the pure, immortal and divine world, away from earth and sea to the highest (element); otherwise they are fettered again by the Erinyes. Therefore, it is necessary to purify one's soul by baths and asceticism.

In 1975 I was interested in finding some background for the conception of a reconciliation of the universe in Christ which we find in the Colossian hymn (Col 1:20). It is unique in the New Testament,[24] since "all things" in this passage clearly includes the "visible and invisible, whether thrones or dominions or principalities or authorities" (Col 1:16). As early as 1930 Ernst Lohmeyer had suggested that the background of this text is to be found in the Jewish fes-

---

[21]*Tusculanae Disputationes* 1:42-3, 18-9; cf. Sextus Empiricus, *Adversus mathematicos* 9:71.

[22]Diels, *Fragmente* 1 356:3ff.; also quoted by Plutarchus, *Moralia* 361c, 607c. Rich evidence in Hellenistic and Hellenistic Jewish writings is given in Eduard Schweizer, " 'Die Elemente der Welt' Gal. 4:3-8; Kol. 2:8-20," in *Verborum Veritas* [Festschrift für Gustav Stählin], ed. O. Böcher and K. Haacker (Wuppertal: Theologischer Verlag Brockhaus, 1970) 245-59; reprinted in Schweizer, *Beiträge zur Theologie des Neuen Testaments* (Zurich: Theologischer Verlag, 1970) 147-63.

[23]Eduard Schweizer, "Versöhnung des Alls," in *Jesus Christus in Historie und Theologie* [Festschrift für Hans Conzelmann], ed. Georg Strecker (Tübingen: J. C. B. Mohr, 1975) 487-501; reprinted in Schweizer, *Neues Testament und Christologie im Werden.* Aufsätze (Göttingen: Vandenhoeck und Ruprecht, 1982) 164-78; abbreviated in Schweizer, *The Letter to the Colossians* (Minneapolis: Augsburg Publishing House, 1982) 128-34.

[24]Eph 1:10 may provide some parallel; yet, the reconciliation of things in heaven and on earth seems to be an eschatological event, not yet fulfilled.

tival of the New Year, especially in the day of reconciliation at the end of the period of penitence following the New Year's Day.[25] But the day of reconciliation is separated from the New Year's festival by ten days; moreover, the terms "redemption, forgiveness of sins and kingdom [of God]" belong to the context of the hymn in Colossians 1:13-14, and not to the hymn itself. According to the hymn it is the resurrection of Jesus that has "reconciled" all things in the universe. It is the author who adds verses 13-14 and reinterprets the hymn by introducing a reference to the death of Jesus on the cross and by understanding, in his subsequent commentary, the universal statement of the hymn as a statement of the reconciliation of the church by the forgiveness of their evil deeds.[26]

In 1960 S. Lyonnet[27] pointed to Philo's interpretation of this festival. Like the Hellenistic authors quoted above, Philo sees the world as in a chaotic disorder, since all the "parts" or "members" (*Spec. Leg.* I.210) of the world (the "elements") fight continually against each other, though without the balanced mixture of the four elements neither man nor universe can exist. Therefore, the high priest, representing the Logos of God and wearing a robe covered with cosmic symbols, represents the universe entering the temple with the high priest in order to be reconciled. The entrance of the high priest not only depicts but actually effects the coming of God's Logos into the world, pacifying the elements, ending the struggle and ordering the cosmos back to a harmony in which there is a stable balance among the different elements so that no one of the elements (earthquakes or inundations or fires or tempests)[28] dominates. Lyonnet, obviously influenced by Lohmeyer's interpretation, connected these Philonic passages with the day of reconciliation. If, however, we must distinguish between the theology of the hymn, which proclaims a cosmic reconciliation, and that of the author to the Colossians who corrects this idea in favor of a reconciliation of the believer whose sins are forgiven, it is possible to see the parallelism between this description of the Jewish New Year's festival and the Colossian hymn. In Philo's text we detect many phrases taken over directly from the Stoic and Pythagorean texts. Thus I was led back to the same texts that I

---

[25]Ernst Lohmeyer, *Die Briefe an die Philipper, und die Kolosser und an Philemon*, Kritisch-exegetischer Kommentar über das Neue Testament, begründet von Heinrich August Wilhelm Meyer 9 (Göttingen: Vandenhoeck und Ruprecht, 1930) ad loc.

[26]The author uses, in Col 1:22, the same Greek verb, also unique in the New Testament (except for Eph 2:16, probably dependent on Colossians), for "reconciling" that he found in the hymn (Col 1:20). It is also the author who added "namely the church" to "the body" (not "his body" or "the body of Christ") in v. 18. See chapter 2(d) above.

[27]Lyonnet, "L'hymne christologique de l'épître aux Colossiens et la fête juive du nouvel an," *Recherches de Science Religieuse* 48 (1960): 93-100. Lyonnet, however, was only interested in the connection of the reconciliation in the cosmos with that of the sinners on the day of reconciliation, as was Ernst Lohmeyer before him.

[28]See Eduard Schweizer, "Versöhnung," 169-70. The main passages are *Spec Leg* 2.188-92 and 1.208-10; *Vit Mos* 2.117-32; *Rer Div Her* 151-53 and 199-201.

found previously in my study of the background of the Colossian heresy. In fact, both ideas were connected in the text mentioned above which provided the best parallel to the terms that describe the heresy in Colossians 2:16-23.

Thus, we can reconstruct what happened in Colossae. First, there were the views of the heretics. They did not doubt the supreme Lordship of the exalted Christ, but they were in doubt about the possibility of the soul ascending to him after death. As many of their contemporaries, from Empedocles and Cicero to Plutarchus and the author of the Pythagorean text, they were anxious to purify their souls during their earthly lives by ascetic rules and purificatory baths, perhaps even by an initiation similar to that known in the mystery religions. The author of the hymn suggested another viewpoint. He was concerned with the chaos of this unstable world, and he proclaimed Christ as the mediator of all creation and as the exalted Lord who had subdued death. It was no longer necessary to repair the chaotic world and to make peace among the elements with each new year, since Christ had done that once and for all. A third perspective was presented by the author of the letter. He quoted the hymn with its praise of the reconciliation granted by Christ, but he restricted it to believers whose sins were forgiven through the death of Jesus on the cross, provided that this faith remained strong and directed towards the goal of a blameless appearance before the judge's seat. Thus, he warned his readers against a false enthusiasm which would assume that all the world was already reconciled and that nothing could threaten them. On the other hand, he quoted some of the appeals of the heretics, but tried to liberate his readers from their fears. Wherever a person "has been raised with him (Christ) through faith," he or she is already living "above" (2:12; 3:1-3). There was no longer any need to prepare for a postmortal ascent of the soul by the keeping of all kinds of ascetic rules concerning food and drink, by special festivals, by self-abasement and many regulations, human precepts and doctrines,[29] because they had already died to the elements of the world with Christ (Col 2:16-23).

It seems clear, then, from this research into the world of religious ideas in Hellenism around the time of the New Testament that, at least as far as the letter to the Colossians and the situation in that congregation is concerned, it was, first of all, a reworking of Platonic and, especially, Pythagorean ideas that formed the background of the theology of both the more "conservative" element and the more "heretical" element of the Colossian church where all kinds of rites had been introduced, and also that of the author of the letter. This, of course, does not prove that the same background is to be seen behind the problems in Galatia or in Corinth and that the same influence shaped the language of Paul. I am not going so far as to exclude the possibility of an incipient Gnosticism in Corinth, although I doubt that it existed. Theologically, of course, it makes little difference whether Platonism or Pythagoreanism or Gnosticism offered the imagery and terminology employed in the New Testament writings. As a historian, however, I should insist that one should always define

---

[29]In contrast to Paul, the author speaks, as do many Pythagorean texts, of *dogmata*.

clearly what he or she means when speaking of Gnostic parallels, and it seems to me that in most parts of the New Testament (with the possible exception of the latest writings), it is sufficient to speak on the one hand of Jewish wisdom speculations and on the other hand of Hellenistic concepts reflective of a middle Platonism as taken over and modified by Pythagoreans, whose influence on Judaism was considerable from the middle of the second century B.C. onward.[30]

I have reviewed in my contribution to the C. K. Barrett *Festschrift* some of the New Testament texts where a Gnostic background is possible and it seems to me that Gnosticism, at least in the sense of a total savior myth, is not detectable. Some of the so-called "Gnostic" ideas seem to be expressions of a generally pessimistic view of this world and a longing for a purer world to which the soul would ascend after death, a view characteristic of Platonic and Pythagorean philosophers. Thus, I would suggest that the New Testament churches and authors on the one hand and later Gnostic systems on the other[31] drew from a common set of ideas. Hence, when in the later 1950s I had to write as my next contribution to Kittel's dictionary an article on *sarx*,[32] I treated the Gnostic evidence after describing the New Testament uses of the word. Ten years later, when I had to write on *psyche*, I discovered on a flight to Berlin just after having mailed my manuscript to the editor a passage in Philo in which the soul is identified with the earth cursed by God, because the soul is, according to this probably pre-Philonic tradition, the cause of all evil in man, tempting him like the serpent in paradise, whereas the mind is neuter, able to judge and to decide between good and bad.[33] This demonstrated that the typically Gnostic anthropology, which evaluated the soul negatively and distinguished it clearly from the innermost self of man, was much older and existed even before Philo.

Once again it is important to note that the historical question of priority does not decide the systematic view. It is certainly possible to describe an event

---

[30]Cf. Aristoboulos (Eusebius, *Praeparatio Evangelica* XIII.12.9), and on him, Martin Hengel, *Judentum und Hellenismus* (Tübingen: J. C. B. Mohr, 1969) 301, 306n392.

[31]See Eduard Schweizer, "Paul's Christology and Gnosticism," in *Paul and Paulinism* [Festschrift" for C. K. Barrett], ed. M. D. Hooker and S. G. Wilson (London: SPCK, 1982) 115-23. For a different view see K. Koschorke, "Eine neugefundene gnostische Gemeindeordnung. Zum Thema Geist und Amt im frühen Christentum," *Zeitschrift für Theologie und Kirche* 76 (1979): 31-60.

[32]Eduard Schweizer, "σάρξ," *Theological Dictionary of the New Testament* 7: 98-151. Cf. my essays, "Rom. 1,3f und der Gegensatz von Fleisch und Geist vor und bei Paulus," *Evangelische Theologie* 15 (1955): 563-71, and "Aufnahme und Korrektur jüdischer Sophiatheologie im Neuen Testament" in *Hören und Handeln* [Festschrift für Ernst Wolf] (Munich: Kaiser-Verlag, 1962) 330-40; reprinted in E. Schweizer, *Neotestamentica* (Zurich: Zwingliverlag, 1963) 180-89 and 210-21.

[33]Philo, *Leg All* 3. 247. See Eduard Schweizer, "ψυχή," *Theological Dictionary* 9:661; see also Schweizer, "σάρξ," *Theological Dictionary* 7:1041.

in a language borrowed from some existing myth in order to define it as given by God and yet emphasize that it is part of real history. Nonetheless, I dealt with the New Testament evidence before dealing with Gnosticism, not merely to indicate my view of the historical problem, but to emphasize that the New Testament message of the descent and ascent of Jesus Christ is more than a borrowed imagery, and that it could not easily be demythologized by separating a Gnostic mythology from an event that could be narrated without any mythical language. Rather the New Testament author who seeks to proclaim the Christ-event (meaning all that had happened in the earthly ministry, death and resurrection of Jesus within our history) as the act of God himself is forced to employ mythical language, whether Greek or Jewish, as the theologian of today would choose some contemporary "mythical" language borrowed perhaps from modern philosophy. He would do so freely and easily, unconcerned with its original use in a particular philosophical or religious context. He would not be adopting a whole "system," a definite myth, or an elaborate world view. Hence, the images to describe the exaltation of Jesus Christ were chosen independently from the imagery that shapes the statements of his preexistence and his incarnation. There are many New Testament passages speaking of Christ's exaltation to God's throne without any hint of his being sent to the earth or his preexistence. Conversely, there are statements about his preexistence combined with his earthly ministry (for instance in the prologue to the Fourth Gospel or in the [baptismal?] formula of 1 Cor 8:6) and statements about his being sent by God combined with his saving death on the cross (Gal 4:4-5; Rom 8:3; Jn 3:16; 1 Jn 4:9; see chapter 2[b]). It is only in a secondary way that the ideas of Christ descending from heaven and ascending again are connected as, for instance, in Philippians 2:6-11 (see chapter 2[d]).

The fact is that God's action precedes all human reaction and, thus, God's action cannot be reduced to a mere "dimension" of man's action or to a description of the religious character of his experience. Therefore, all mythical language must secure the "objectivity" of God's acts before and outside of all our human deeds, thoughts, and feelings. This is central for Paul. Three times using the same phrase and in similar contexts he distinguishes between a life "according to the flesh," in which man is the subject who lives his life oriented to the normative principles of the "flesh," and a life "by (or through) the Spirit" (or the promise of God), in which God's Spirit is the subject that determines a man's life.[34] This means that God's acting on man cannot be dissolved into a language of human self-understanding, even when that self-understanding is given by God. For Paul, man does not simply live his life according to the norms of the Spirit as does the true believer; rather, he owes his very existence to the Spirit.

This is exactly what Ernst Käsemann emphasized in his famous lecture published in 1954,[35] He approached the problem of the historical Jesus by

---

[34]See Rom 8:13-4; Gal 4:23 (cf. 5:18); Phil 3:3; Schweizer, "σάρξ," 7, 132.

[35]Ernst Käsemann, "Das Problem des historischen Jesus," in *Exegetische Versuche und Besinnungen*, 2 vols. (Göttingen: Vandenhoeck und Ruprecht, 1967) 1:187-214.

demonstrating that when one compared life-of-Jesus research in the first two decades of this century with contemporary research, it is clear that liberal and conservative scholars had done an about face! It was now the "liberals" who (following the lead of Bultmann) stressed the importance of the Christological confessions, whereas "conservatives" defended, to a certain degree, research on the historical Jesus and his relation to the later Christologies. Even in this first essay Käsemann argued for taking much more seriously the "once" and the "once for all" of God's presence in Jesus. About ten years later, he outlined his position in strict opposition to a Christian theology which was but a cover for a philosophical understanding of the world and existence in which Jesus was merely a precipitative factor for a particular way of understanding the world and Christ was merely a kind of symbol or "chiffre." He expressed his conviction that the place of God before, outside, and over all human faith could only be taught in "a Christology distinguished unambiguously from both ecclesiology and anthropology." It should be the answer of those who know clearly about the "priority of Christ to those who belong to him" and "the *extra nos* (outside of us) of the gospel message."[36]

The same interest led me to a somewhat different understanding of Paul's concept of the body of Christ. I agree completely with Käsemann that the term "body" is for Paul primarily a means of communication. The human body may define a person from head to toe, and "body" describes everything that is held together by the skin. But the human body possesses eyes to see, ears to hear, hands to receive or to give, feet to move toward or away from somebody or something else. In this sense, "body" is understood as a subject that communicates with other persons or things, and it is this understanding that is most relevant for Paul in his use of this term. I also understand very well Käsemann's fear of an ecclesiology that would replace Christology, in which the church as the institution of salvation would take the place of Christ himself and actually dispense with him. It was, however, precisely the undeniable priority of Christ in the New Testament, and especially in Paul's letters, that led me to understand the body of Christ primarily as the body of Jesus crucified (Rom 7:4 and the passages dealing with the Lord's Supper; cf. Col 1:22 and Eph 2:13-14). This is the "realm" of salvation and lordship into which the believer is brought by means of baptism (1 Cor 12:12-13). I am aware of the danger of a direct identification of the church with that body crucified, of an understanding of the church as the "Christus prolongatus" (the "prolonged" or the "lasting Christ"), in which Christ has been definitively replaced by his church. And yet, passages like 1 Corinthians 12:12-13 clearly show that in Paul's theology the "body of Christ" is not simply the result of a uniting action of believers but is a given reality not created by human faith and obedience, but offered as the place of real life by Christ himself to those who are willing to receive his gift.

---

[36]Ernst Käsemann, "Sackgassen im Streit um den historischen Jesus," in *Exegetische Versuche* 2:31-68.

Similarly, according to John 1:51, Christ is the "Son of Man" depicted as the new Jacob-Israel (cf. Gen 28:12) and according to John 15:1 he is the vine that embraces all believers (who can do "nothing without him," 15:4-5!) as its branches. Since the vine is *the* symbol for Israel (Ps 80:9 et al.) and since a contemporary first-century Jewish text even speaks of Israel as a cosmic vine whose roots reach to the abyss and whose branches to the sky (or the heaven),[37] it seems obvious that Christ is seen by John as the new Israel in whom all believers find real life.

In the early 1960s, I became better acquainted with my British colleagues and their hypothesis that the Son of Man title was used in a corporate sense (see chapter 4[b]), and though I never went so far as they did, I suggested that in John 15 the concept of Israel as the vine of God had been used to describe the significance of Jesus for his church. How and how far this understanding of the total dependence of the disciples on their Lord in whom alone they are able to live and to bear "fruit" should be combined with the view of Jesus as the Son of man is difficult to say. The identification of the vine Israel with the son of man in Ps 80:16 (at least in the Septuagint, but also detectable in the background of the Hebrew text) and the appearance of the Son of Man title in John 1:51, where Jesus is depicted as the new Jacob, suggests the existence of some combination of the two concepts in the pre-Johannine tradition.[38] The image of the vine embracing all the branches, giving them their life and causing them to bear fruit, is parallel to that of the human body embracing all of its members and enabling them to render their respective services. The difference lies in the Johannine concentration on Israel as compared with the universalistic view found in Paul.

Since Gnosticism offers no parallel to the "body of Christ" concept before Mani in the third century A.D., except where the knowledge of Paul is to be presupposed,[39] it seems highly probable that the pre-Johannine "vine" and the Pauline "body" are two ideas that would not have been developed independently. If this is the case, the "narrower" idea of Christ's significance for Israel, which is very much in line with Jewish ideas of the cosmic significance of the people of God and of the patriarch determining the whole history of his tribe, would be the earlier level, and Paul's emphasis on the significance of Christ for the world as a whole be a further development of the same basic conception. The influence of Hellenistic cosmic speculations with regard to Zeus,

---

[37]Pseudo-Philo, *Antiquitates Biblicae* 12.8.

[38]See Charles H. Dodd, *The Interpretation of the Fourth Gospel* (Cambridge, 1953) 411.

[39]Eduard Schweizer, "σῶμα," *Theological Dictionary* 7: 1070-71, 1090-92, and now especially Karl Martin Fischer, *Tendenz und Absicht des Epheserbriefs*, Forschungen zur Literatur des Alten und Neuen Testaments 111 (Göttingen: Vandenhoeck und Ruprecht, 1973) 48-78; also Schweizer, "σῶμα," in *Exegetisches Wörterbuch zum Neuen Testament*, ed. Horst Balz and Gerhard Schneider (Stuttgart: Kohlhammer, 1983) 776-79.

heaven, or Logos as the head of the universe in Colossians and Ephesians would present still another development.[40] From a totally different approach Cilliers Breytenbach has recently concluded similarly that the doctrine of a reconciliation of the universe in the Colossian hymn is a further development due to these cosmic speculations of the original Pauline doctrine and not vice versa.[41] All this lies, of course, in the area of historical truth and can be maintained only with some degree of probability, never with absolute certainty. Nonetheless, if this sketch of the history of the "body of Christ" concept is more or less correct, it shows again how important it was to the early church to proclaim a salvation rooted in the acts of God in the history of Israel and of humankind as clearly preceding the believing and the preaching of the church.

(h) The Significance of the Earthly Jesus for the Kerygma of the Church

In 1964-1966 I wrote and typed my commentary on Mark[42] (the service of secretaries was in that time not yet available for private research!). At this time, besides teaching New Testament, I was serving as president of the University of Zurich, and during those days I was compelled to engage in an even more comprehensive critical review of Bultmann's theology. This silent dialogue with my teacher, characterized by both gratitude and doubting, continued during the fall of 1966, when finding myself in Japan with quite a bit of free time and almost no books at hand, I tried to summarize why Jesus was so important to me and, therefore, according to my understanding, to the church. On my return to Zurich I read extensively from the available literature and set out to flesh out more completely that first sketch of what would become my book published in English as *Jesus*.[43] It was a period that saw a plethora of books about Jesus. In 1967 Norman Perrin's *Rediscovering the Teaching of Jesus* was published. Herbert Braun's *Jesus* followed in 1969, and two years later Ernst Fuchs published his book *Jesus, Wort und Tat*.[44] All of these would prove that Bultmann's thesis that the mere "that" (namely, the mere knowledge of the fact of the crucifixion of Jesus) would suffice for the church as it had sufficed for Paul (see chapter 1[a]) could not be maintained.

Bultmann's decision to produce an interpretation of the Fourth Gospel in his grand commentary was the inevitable result of his own theological per-

---

[40]Eduard Schweizer, "σῶμα," in *Theological Dictionary* 7: 1037; Schweizer, *Colossians*, 58-59. For an opposing view, see Fischer, *Tendenz*.

[41]J. Cilliers Breytenbach, *Katallage. Eine Studie zur paulinischen Soteriologie* (Habilitationsschrift, Munich, 1985).

[42]Eduard Schweizer, *The Good News According to Mark* (Atlanta: John Knox Press, 1970).

[43]Eduard Schweizer, *Jesus* (Atlanta: John Knox Press, 1971).

[44]Norman Perrin, *Rediscovering the Teaching of Jesus* (London: SCM Press, 1967); Herbert Braun, *Jesus. Der Mann aus Nazareth und seine Zeit* (Stuttgart: Kreuz Verlag, 1969); Ernst Fuchs, *Jesus, Wort und Tat* (Tübingen: J. C. B. Mohr, 1971).

spective and the notion that the Jesus of the Fourth Gospel is more representative of the perspective of the post-Easter kerygma than the Jesus of the Synoptics. The fact that I was asked to interpret the Synoptics[45] is certainly less intentional; however, this commission met with my interest and enabled me to address some of my central concerns to them. Among New Testament scholars form criticism had been replaced by a new interest in the history of the traditions within a Synoptic text, and then by redaction criticism, which investigated the theological interest of the last redactor, the author of the gospel. At this time most of the books about Jesus (with which I dealt in my first lecture) were interested in getting back to the authentic sayings and deeds of Jesus. Authors like Herbert Braun or Ernst Fuchs were especially eager to find the kerygma of the post-Easter church in the preaching and activity of the earthly Jesus; others like M. Machovec or F. Belo drew a definite distinction between the earthly Jesus and later developments, that is, the post-Easter kerygma which in their opinion neglected or even distorted much of what Jesus sought to convey to humankind.

When I worked on the interpretation of Mark (and later on that of Matthew and Luke) my first question was, naturally enough: what does the evangelist want to teach us? More and more I came to see Mark as a real and formidable theologian. The truth that a gospel is not merely a report of facts, but a missionary appeal intended to announce the author's conviction that in the deeds and sayings he reports in his gospel God himself wants to meet and save human beings and to build up his people is to be taken very seriously. The effort to isolate the theology of Mark (or of Matthew or Luke) by studying the arrangement of the traditions that each author had at hand and the short redactional notices or links between two passages he composed proved to be an important contribution to understanding the different theological approaches of the New Testament authors. Of course, this requires that we ask whether or not the evangelist himself has understood Jesus correctly.

The answer to this question is even more difficult to ascertain. First, it is difficult to know what stories or sayings are authentic. There is a kind of consensus that while there are almost no details about which we can be absolutely sure, there is an overall view of Jesus' ministry manifesting some very clear features that will stand the test of the critical historian (see chapter 1[b]). Second, and more important, is another problem: What does it mean to understand Jesus correctly? I had learned from Bultmann that it is impossible to understand Jesus without getting involved. Getting involved means understanding Jesus in relation to one's own situation, questions, problems, and hopes. Thus, by necessity, any understanding must be one-sided, emphasizing one section of the whole, and the modern reader can only come to a right understanding of Jesus by listening to the manifold testimony of the different authors. Each of the Synoptics lends its unique witness to the choir of the New

---

[45]See Eduard Schweizer, *The Good News According to Mark/Matthew/Luke* (Atlanta: John Knox Press, 1970/1976/1984).

Testament writers and each underlines the necessity to check any one theology time and again over against the words and deeds of Jesus himself, the Jesus who is the central focus of the preaching of the New Testament church and the authors of each of the New Testament documents.

Thus, when a year after completing my commentary on Mark I set out to write a book about Jesus, I departed from previous patterns and included in it the history of the church's developing understanding of Jesus. Only the first part of the book speaks of the earthly ministry of Jesus, his death and his resurrection; the other five parts describe the apocalyptic hope of the church for his parousia, the developing understanding of Jesus in terms of his exaltation to a heavenly Lordship and eventually of his preexistence and incarnation, the importance of his death for the church and for the world, the significance of his earthly ministry as the gospels see it, and finally, some new developments that occurred in the time of transition from the New Testament period to the church of the second century.

The decision to write the book in this way was, of course, a decision that I owe again to the influence of Bultmann. He felt himself to have been best understood by Herbert Braun, because in his book Braun had detected the same kerygma in the life of Jesus that Bultmann had found in Paul and John. But had not Bultmann taught us that it was only the "kerygma," the word of the witnesses proclaiming Jesus as the Christ, that would lead to real faith? Without their testimony we should never detect God's saving coming in Jesus by our own insight. Had he not told us that it was futile to try to go behind this word to a Jesus not yet interpreted by the faith of those who were won by him? The scholar could and would do so, of course, and it might help him to understand some details more adequately, but it was not really essential to faith.

I have tried and am still trying to take this thesis seriously insofar as it reminds us that it was only the events of Easter and Pentecost that revealed Jesus as the Christ of God. Such a view states unmistakably that neither the religious teacher nor the infectious example of a believer in God is the basis of salvation. That basis is only to be found in the word that preaches Jesus as the Christ. It may well be that the tradition has exaggerated the disciples' blindness and their lack of understanding of the claim of Jesus; nevertheless, it is a fact that no disciple was present to fulfill one of the first duties of first-century piety—to care for the burial of the body of the crucified Jesus. It was an outsider who did it. Thus, as I said in the first chapter, it would be an illusion to think that if we could just go back to wander with the earthly Jesus through Galilee, listen to his authentic words, and see his authentic deeds, we would then detect God in him. To paraphrase the words of Ernst Käsemann, a Christian way of speaking of Jesus can never become merely a cover for a political or social program, even if it is the best program of all, if the figure of Jesus is seen merely as a factor that prompts a particular process of thought, and the title Christ becomes little more than a kind of symbol or "chiffre."

(i) The Kerygma an Ideology?

If we grant a final authority to the kerygma of the church, does this not lead to an ideology that has to be accepted simply because of the authority of the church, just as one would swallow a medication because of the authority of the physician? There is no doubt that this is a very real danger, and it must be avoided. Yet two logically connected considerations demand our attention.

First, in countries where the old European tradition of one country, one church (or as in Switzerland and Germany, one Protestant and one Catholic church) is no longer living, I have come to see churches from various Christian traditions working side by side. This is especially true in Great Britian and the United States. In Australia I taught among a faculty and student body in which Presbyterians, Congregationalists, Methodists, Episcopalians and Jesuits were involved together in preparation for the ministry. In 1966 I suggested that the Neukirchener Verlag publish an Evangelical (meaning "Protestant!")—Catholic Commentary on the New Testament with annual workshops for all the authors. In the many years of cooperation in these meetings—the best team work of which I know in our field—I have come to see how much the situation of a church, its specific problems and dangers, its experiences both good and bad, determine the way in which it has to proclaim the truth of the gospel. From the beginning the "Wirkungsgeschichte," the history of the impact a text made and of its reception by different readers throughout the history of the church was emphasized, and though a New Testament scholar is no specialist in this field and can give but a fragmentary survey of the history of interpretation, this approach proved very fruitful.

When I wrote my interpretation of Colossians in this series,[46] I was so aware of my shortcomings as a church historian that I was very reluctant even to start the research in this area. Thus, the history of the reception of the text appears in the last chapter. When I did do this research, however, it was so interesting and it revealed so many new insights into the text that I should have liked to have begun the whole commentary over again, introducing what I had learned from the history of the interpretation of this text much more directly into the verse-by-verse interpretation. This is what Ulrich Luz, one of my former students, did in his commentary on Matthew,[47] and it became obvious how much the truth of a text comes to light in the long history of its being understood and misunderstood, and even more in the long history of its being lived out by those who have read it. There are sayings in the Sermon on the Mount, for example, that were originally understood in a literal way, but gradually came to be seen in a mitigated sense. This caused a movement in the church towards a more radical obedience, and since such a response was seen as impossible for all members of the church, it was the monks and nuns who tried to fulfill the commandments of the Lord literally. In the Reformation this led to the insight that Jesus did not distinguish between disciples who were to be radically obedient

[46]See Eduard Schweizer, *Der Brief an die Kolosser*, Evangelisch-Katholischer Kommentar zum Neuen Testament 12 (Zurich: Benziger; Neukirchen: Neukirchener Verlag, 1976; 2nd. ed., 1980); for the English translation see n. 23 above.

[47]Ulrich Luz, *Das Evangelium nach Matthäus* 1, Teilband Mt 1-7, Evangelisch-Katholischer Kommentar zum Neuen Testament 1 (Zurich: Benziger; Neukirchen: Neukirchener Verlag, 1985).

and disciples who were not. While radical obedience was expected from all, Luther argued that there are two realms—the private realm in which such obedience is possible, and the public realm (in which one must act as a king or a judge or even a parent) in which the commandments of the Sermon on the Mount are not directly applicable. This view prompted protests from Calvinists who noted (correctly again) that Jesus did not set aside some areas in which his commandments could be disregarded. The history of these interpretive controversies sharpens the eyes of the interpreter and enables him to become aware of the pitfalls that threaten our understanding when we neglect that history and fail to see how the text has been understood in the lives of those who have read it before us. We must learn from their exegetical and practical understandings in order to avoid their misunderstandings. In some way, the experience of God, deemphasized very much by Karl Barth in favor of the word of God, is coming to the forefront once again. In my view this is not a problem, provided that all experience is checked by the measuring stick of the primary experiences of those who speak to us in the New Testament. Though we have to express the truth of the New Testament using different language, the words of the primary witnesses must dominate and determine our words. In the same way, their experiences must be the binding models by which we evaluate our contemporary experiences.

The second consideration concerns the different levels of language about which I spoke in chapter 2[c]. In an essay in 1961[48] I saw in the idea of the reconciliation of the universe found in Colossians 1:20 the expression of an enthusiasm that had allowed itself to be swept away to the point of formulating heretical statements. Since that time I have learned, especially from my Roman Catholic friends, to see the difference between the language of adoration in a divine service, addressed to God himself and born out of the common faith of the congregation assembled there, and the language of teaching, addressed to fellow Christians and/or unbelievers in order to warn them against errors and to guide them towards a deeper understanding of the faith. Thus, my judgment changed in a first draft of an interpretation of the Colossian hymn and, later on, in my commentary.[49] This insight has been significantly strengthened by the results of modern research on the parables of Jesus (mentioned briefly in chapter 3[a]), which we owe to Amos Wilder, Robert Funk, Dan Via, Norman Perrin, John Crossan, and others in the USA, and to Ernst

---

[48]Eduard Schweizer, "Die Kirche als Leib Christi in den paulinischen Antilegomena," *Theologische Literaturzeitung* 86 (1961): 241-56; reprinted in Schweizer, *Neotestamentica* (Zurich, 1963) 293-316.

[49]Eduard Schweizer, *Evangelisch-Katholischer Kommentar zum Neuen Testament. Vorarbeiten,* Heft 1 (Zurich: Benziger; Neukirchen: Neukirchener Verlag, 1969) 24-39; *Der Brief an die Kolosser,* ad loc.

Fuchs, Eberhard Jüngel, and also to Hans Weder, one of my students, in Europe.[50]

As early as 1968, when my book on Jesus appeared, I sensed the importance of the findings of all these colleagues. Thus, the title of chapter 2—"Jesus: The Man Who Fits No Formula"—became, for my understanding of Jesus and the further development of this understanding, perhaps the most important part of that paperback. It expressed the truth that in his preaching—comprised almost exclusively of parables as far as the proclamation of God and his kingdom, of sin and salvation, of death and resurrection was concerned—and in all his actions or experiences a reality was revealed that could not be captured by doctrinal formulae. What the Johannine tradition of the speeches of Jesus had taught me about his being the true vine, the good shepherd, the bread of life, and so forth was suddenly confirmed in a very different way by the Synoptic parables. Their function was not to clarify a definition of God, his kingdom or his attitude towards men by connecting a statement about God with a comparable statement about our earthly reality. The building block of the parable is not the simile, because a direct correlation of cosmos and divine Logos as the Hellenists saw it does not exist. The building block of the parable is, rather, the metaphor.[51] What the speeches of Jesus in John express in a very pointed way, the Synoptic parables also say: there is nothing in what we call reality which can be compared to the reality of God. He is so different from all we know that neither human words nor human images are able to adequately capture him. In a parable, Jesus starts from everyday experiences, not to define God and his acts, but to initiate, on a different level, a chain of experiences in which God himself moves towards the hearers and enlivens them.

In my dissertation I was forced to admit that the so-called Johannine parables were not similes, but direct language to be taken seriously. Modern research on the Synoptic parables showed that they were not so very far away

---

[50]Cf., for instance, John Dominic Crossan, *In Parables* (New York: Harper and Row, 1973); Robert W. Funk, *Language, Hermeneutic, and Word of God* (New York: Harper and Row, 1966); Funk, *Parables and Presence* (Philadelphia: Fortress Press, 1982); Wolfgang Harnisch, *Die Gleichniserzählungen Jesu,* Uni Taschenbücher 1343 (1985); Werner Georg Kümmel, "Jesusforschung seit 1965," *Theologische Rundschau* 43 (1978): 120-42, and 47 (1982): 353-66; Paul Ricoeur and Eberhard Jüngel, *Metapher, Beihefte zur Evangelischen Theologie* (Munich: Kaiser, 1974); Dan O. Via, *The Parables of Jesus* (Philadelphia: Fortress Press, 1967); Hans Weder, *Die Gleichnisse Jesu als Metaphern,* Forschungen zur Religion und Literatur des Alten und Neuen Testaments 120 (Tübingen: Vandenhoeck und Ruprecht, 1978); Claus Westermann, *Vergleiche und Gleichnisse im Alten und Neuen Testament.* Calwer Theologische Monographien A 14 (Stuttgart: Calwer Verlag, 1984); Amos N. Wilder, *Early Christian Rhetoric* (Cambridge: Harvard University Press, 1971); idem, *Jesus' Parables and the War of Myths* (Philadelphia: Fortress Press, 1982). More literature is cited in my article "Jesus Christus" in *Theologische Realenzyklopädie* 10.3. Cf. now the excellent chapter on the metaphoric language in Weder, *Neutestamentliche Hermeneutik* (Zurich: Theologischer Verlag, 1986) 155-285.

[51]Schweizer, *Jesus,* 26-30.

from this, for a metaphor is also a specific form of direct language which describes reality in a new way.[52] For instance, the classical example of a metaphor "Achilles is a lion" certainly does not simply define Achilles since he is a human being, not a lion, but it describes him in a way that is the only important one in the text. A good metaphor is not vague; it is a very precise characterization. If I describe a person as "icy cold," this is not a definition (since her temperature would be somewhere around 98.6 degrees), but in the context of a discussion about her relations to other people it expresses the way she reacts to other people much more precisely than if I had spoken of the difficulty she experiences in relating to other people. Relating these thoughts to the word of God, Jesus' use of parables shows that there is no earthly reality comparable to that of God, and because of this no human word can define God. Though we can teach about God, erecting some parameters not to be crossed, it is impossible to teach God; it is, however, possible to speak of him and of his coming in a parable, in which his and his kingdom's coming is related to experiences that characterize our world.

In some way, this justifies Bultmann's thesis that it is impossible to speak of God without speaking of how he becomes real in our existence, and that, ultimately, we are only able to speak of the way he meets us. This is true insofar as it is impossible to speak of God in a totally detached way, as if he had nothing to do with us. Unless we are moved by a parable we cannot understand it. Thus, the parables of Jesus often speak of how God encounters humanity and of humanity's reaction (for example, the merchant who found the one precious pearl), but they also speak of the life of God's kingdom before it reaches us and outside all our reactions (the seed that sprouts while the farmer is sleeping or the mustard seed that grows to a tree). Even more important, as I discussed in chapter 3, the surprising elements in almost every parable of Jesus point to the narrator himself. The truth of a parable is not a general truth, true everywhere and in any time. It becomes true in the teaching of Jesus itself and in his whole life and death and resurrection.[53] Faith can never give up praising God and all his actions, even those that happened long before the believer heard of them and was moved by them.

In summary, the use of the parables proves that the kingdom of God is not an idea. It is life itself. The parable tells us about the way God is living and coming into relation with us, and it is impossible to capture the story of the parable in a dogmatic statement that the reader could preserve apart from the parable. There is no "moral of the story" that would summarize the meaning of the parable forever. A parable can repeat its message from a totally different

---

[52]Jüngel and Ricoeur, as quoted by Weder, *Die Gleichnisse*, 64, 61.

[53]Some examples are given in chapter 3(a). Other illustrations include the woman who invites all her friends (and, as a boy in Sunday School remarked, spends more money for coffee and biscuits than she found), Lk 15:9; the welcome of the father to the prodigal son, Lk 15:22-3; the callousness of priest and Levite, Lk 10:31-32. Cf. Schweizer, *Jesus*, 28-9; Schweizer, *The Good News According to Luke*, 250-52, 382.

angle tomorrow and differently again the day after tomorrow, because it is the living God himself who meets us in the parables of Jesus and meets us in the immediate context of our lives today and tomorrow and the day after.[54]

(j) Jesus—the Parable of God[55]

It is most helpful, then, to understand Jesus as the parable of God in his gracious presence. (See chapter 1[b].) On the one hand, this says that reducing the life and death of Jesus to the mere fact of his crucifixion (a la Bultmann) will not suffice, since it is impossible to reduce a parable to a doctrinal statement. Jesus cannot be reduced to the doctrine of justification without losing decisive elements of the truth. A belief in Jesus that does not include the whole of his preaching and his work—that is, a belief that would not be "stamped" by the life and death of Jesus of Nazareth—would not be real faith. This is the justification of all attempts at Christological reflection that begin with the earthly Jesus and find in him the impulse for and the basis of a new way of life. Marxists and the representatives of a theology of liberation teach us never to forget that it is impossible to meet the real Jesus without taking the political and social situation—that is, the wants and needs of all our fellow human beings—seriously. (See chapter 1[c].) On the other hand, a parable is nothing in and of itself. The story of a shepherd who finds his lost sheep or of a woman who is baking bread is certainly not in and of itself very significant. Without the convincing authority of the storyteller who tells the hearer that this is how the kingdom of God is coming to him or her through this parable, the parable remains senseless. In the same way, the life and death of Jesus of Nazareth as a whole remains senseless, so long as it is not proclaimed as the coming of God and his kingdom, as the announcement of God's astonishing, revolutionizing and saving presence.

The disciples were overwhelmed by the life and death of Jesus and after Easter and Pentecost came to understand it as God's presence. Without their telling of the story, in the form of gospels or in the form of epistles, it would remain meaningless in the same way as does a parable that is not heard as the announcement of the kingdom of God. This lends justification to the view that all Christological reflection must start from the kerygma of the church after Easter and Pentecost. From Teilhard de Chardin's history of salvation up to

---

[54]Compare Mt 18:12-14 (in the context of an exhortation to be concerned about church members that are in danger of being lost) with the different message in Lk 15:4-7.

[55]Edward Schillebeeckx, *Jesus, Die Geschichte von einem Lebenden* (Freiburg: Herder, 1980) 555; Eberhard Jüngel, *Gott als Geheimnis der Welt* (Tübingen: J. C. B. Mohr, 1977) 491, 495; Dorothee Sölle, *Stellvertretung: ein Kapitel Theologie nach dem "Tode Gottes"* (Stuttgart: Kreuz-Verlag, 1967) 183; cf. Weder, *Gleichnisse,* 299: Theologically the identification of Jesus with Christ is the basic metaphor. For a different view see Ben-Chorin, *Jesus im Judentum* (Wuppertal: Theologischer Verlag, 1970) 74: "the parable of Israel."

the recent presentations of process theology, there is a new emphasis on the objective change that has taken place since Jesus Christ, a change that is before and outside of all subsequent human reactions.

This also implies a new understanding of what "trinity" means. Gradually I have learned from many of my colleagues, first from Eberhard Jüngel's *Gottes Sein ist im Werden (God's Being is in the Becoming)*, then more and more from the North American and European research on the parables as a specific form of language, to see in Trinitarian doctrine not a definition of God but rather a narrative report about a living person. The anthropomorphisms of the Old Testament, in which God is described like a human person, and the reluctance to give him a name in Judaism, are expressions of that insight. The image of a person, therefore, recommended itself to Israel and to the church of the New Testament. First, it is the image of one person because God is doubtless only one. And yet, a person is not imaginable without eyes to see and ears to hear, in other words, without communication with the world outside of it. Is it not better, therefore, to speak of two persons, of father and son? As the love of the father flows to the son and comes back in the love of the son, so God himself is living love from all eternity, long before the earth was created. If we refrain from efforts to define God in a mathematical way but instead point to his being alive, then we have to describe him in the image of father and son, understood as the two poles of a dynamic and continually living love. But again, this would not be enough, since God is never self-complacent. Even human love is never totally restricted to two persons. It always emanates and permeates it surroundings. Two parents that love each other create the atmosphere in which a baby can grow. Indeed, without that love it would even die physically. Thus, would it not be even better to use the image of three persons, Father, Son and Holy Spirit, when speaking of the truly living God?[56]

Returning to the idea of Jesus as the parable of God, we might understand better the diversity of the New Testament Christologies, or "Jesus Christ in the Manifold Testimony of the New Testament," as reads the subtitle of my book about Jesus. They are not simply "compulsory" doctrines to be accepted. They are expressions of the truth by which we may meet the living God speaking to us today. Thus, the concept of the atoning death of Jesus is a very central metaphorical way of speaking, which becomes true wherever human beings experience, individually or collectively, liberation from guilt in such a way that they will never forget "what the weight of sin is" apart from the atonement. The concept of ransom is another of these figurative sayings that becomes true wherever persons are freed to a new life from any power that has

---

[56]"Economic" and "immanent trinity" may be distinguished rationally but not separated from each other: Eberhard Jüngel, *Entsprechungen. Gott-Wahrheit-Mensch* (Munich: Kaiser-Verlag, 1980) 275. See also Jüngel, *Gott*, 506-507. For Dietrich Bonhoeffer, Hans Küng, Jürgen Moltmann, Karl Rahner, Edward Schillebeeckx, Paul Tillich, and T. F. Torrance, see evidence in Schweizer, *Jesusdarstellungen*, 146; cf. Schweizer, "Zur Trinitätsfrage," *Internationale Kirchliche Zeitschrift* 72 (1982): 69-71.

enslaved them (be it drugs, greed, complacency or any of the thousands of powers separating humanity from God and his kingdom). The concept of dying and rising with Christ is a third image expressing the significance of Jesus' death. It becomes true wherever his life and death shape and determine the life and death of his disciple. In all three of these forms and in many others that could be drawn from other parts of the New Testament, the emphasis lies on God's act in Jesus' death and resurrection as preceding and causing all human answers to it. Not one of them is really understandable without the testimony of the witnesses who have detected God's decisive work in Jesus, especially in his death and resurrection, or without being "fleshed out" by a knowledge of who Jesus was in his whole earthly existence from its beginning to the final exaltation to God. This means that a comprehensive New Testament Christology must be broad enough and hospitable enough to allow room for all these different interpretations. It does not mean that it must necessarily repeat all of them. As long as we cannot reinterpret them in a meaningful way for people today, the mere repetition of them will not help. This does not mean that we should not value and evaluate the different options, giving prominence to an imagery which is especially meaningful for our time and place and leaving others more on the periphery. It does mean, however, that we must be totally open to all the different testimonies of the New Testament, eagerly expecting their message in a new way in which we have not yet heard it. And it does mean that the conviction that God himself is speaking to us in Jesus, in his table fellowship with tax collectors as well as in his appearances as the risen Lord, must be expressed in a credible way, and that significant words like "righteousness of God," "salvation," and "life with God" are equally well interpreted by the whole "parable," the life and work of Jesus, in which all this became true. Again, the result is clear: the pendulum has to swing from the kerygma to Jesus of Nazareth and from him back to the kerygma. In a culture in which the claim of the church that Jesus is the Christ is still known even where it is not accepted as true, the reverse movement from Jesus to the kerygma and then back to Jesus is also possible, though the other sequence is, in my view, the one that most clearly accentuates the truth.

In some way, I have come full circle and find myself back where I started as a young *doctorand*. The circle, in spite of many breaches, bulges, and crooked lines, is more or less closed. What could have been guessed from the results of my dissertation (though I failed to do so) has been unfolded in an unexpected way by the findings of others. God is a reality compared with which all that we call "reality" is but an image and a feeble copy. Compared with his love all that we call love is but an emanation of God's own love. Therefore, only God's own engagement of us, as it has happened in Jesus Christ, is able to bridge the gap between God and man. And it is only his engagement of us again, as it has happened in the coming of the Holy Spirit, which is able to open human beings to faith. Both of these ways in which God engages us reach us in the churches' proclamation of Jesus as the Christ.

An old ballad by the German poet Gustav Schwab tells of a rider who crossed the ice-covered lake of Constance one foggy day without realizing it. When he had reached the other shore and heard what he had done and realized how many times he could have drowned and how many times he had escaped the abyss, the shock killed him and he fell dead on the spot. I can only hope that the reader who knows, perhaps even better than I, of all the chasms over which I have just jumped and all the thin ice on which I have been treading, will not experience the same fate as that unfortunate rider.

INDEX

2. Modern Authors

3. Subjects

Abba, 49-50
Apocalypticism, 16-17, 48
Atonement, 69-70, 89; see also Jesus, death
Body of Christ, 24-25, 47, 79-81

Canon, 12
Christology
 docetic/ebionitic, 29, 35, 41
 implicit, 2, 32, 49-50, 59
 plurality, 9-10, 12, 69-71, 82-83, 89
Church, 66-67, 79
Communication, 31, 54, 71-72, 89
Conscientious objectors, 68
Corporate personality, 47, 80

Demythologization, 6-7, 78
Discipleship, 34-36, 71
Disclosure, 50-55

Easter; see Jesus, resurrection
Ecumenism, 68
Empedocles, 73-76
Experience, 31, 35, 40-41, 62-63, 73, 86

Faith, 51-54, 91
 as journey, 40-41

Galilee, 30-33
Gnosticism, 22, 29, 41-42, 72-78
God
 dead, 5
 extra nos (outside of us), 2-3, 19, 79, 87, 89
 not teachable, 65, 87
Grace, 69

History, 3; see also Salvation history
Hitler, 66, 68, 71; see also National Socialism
"I am . . . ," 42-43, 64-65, 86-87
Ideology, 83-84, cf. 89-90
Israel, 27, 39, 47, 80

Jerusalem, 30-33, 40
Jesus
 ascent/descent, 22-23, 78
 death, 13, 17, 19, 24, 27, 32, 35-37, 42, 50-52
  its meaning, 18, 69-72, 89
 exaltation, 22-23, 42, 70, 78
 humiliation, 22-23, 70

incarnation, 24-26, 39, 78
lordship, 16-19, 23, 50-57, 65-69, 76
ministry on earth, 2-8, 12-13, 17, 23, 25-28, 51, 55-56, 59, 78, 81-91
miracles, 33-34, 37
parable of God, 88-91
parousia, 15-17, 23, 30
preexistence, 20, 23-25, 78
resurrection, 1, 4-5, 7, 9-10, 13, 15, 17, 24-25, 27, 32, 83
titles, 57

John, 28, 34, 41-43
Justification, 2, 4, 43, 88
Kerygma, 1, 8-14, 44-49, 55-56, 88-91
Language, different levels, 21, 31, 65, 78
Law, 27, 38-39
Liberation Theology, 10, 88
Logos, 20, 24, 25, 75, 81, 86
Love, 5, 11, 38-39, 67, 90
Luke, 40-41

Mark, 35-37, 82
Matthew, 37-40
Marxism, 6-7, 88
Messiah, 44-45, 49-52
Metaphor, 86-87
Mission to the nations, 24
Myth, 78

National Socialism, 59; see also Hitler
Natural Theology, 61, 64
Parables, 31, 65, 85-91; see also "I am . . . " (for John)
Paul, 27-28
Philo, 74-77
 pseudo-Philo, 80
Plurality; see Christology, Political/social engagement
Political/social engagement, 5-10, 60, 65-69, 83, 88
 plurality of approaches, 67-69
Process Theology, 11, 89
Pythagoreans, 73-77

Q, 29-33

Religion(s), 61-64
Resurrection, 52-55; see also Jesus, resurrection